Voices of 1966
MEMORIES OF ENGLAND'S WORLD CUP

Voices of 1966
MEMORIES OF ENGLAND'S WORLD CUP

Compiled by
Norman Shiel

TEMPUS

First published 2000
Copyright © Norman Shiel, 2000

Tempus Publishing Limited
The Mill, Brimscombe Port,
Stroud, Gloucestershire, GL5 2QG

ISBN 0 7524 2045 3

Typesetting and origination by
Tempus Publishing Limited
Printed in Great Britain by
Midway Clark Printing, Wiltshire

Also available from Tempus Publishing

Birmingham City FC	Tony Matthews	0 7524 1862 9
Bristol City FC 1894-1967	Tom Hopegood/David Woods	0 7524 2040 2
Bristol Rovers FC	Mike Jay	0 7524 1150 0
Burnley FC 1882-1968	Ray Simpson	0 7524 1520 4
Bury FC	Peter Cullen	0 7524 1526 3
Cardiff City FC 1971-1993	Richard Shepherd	0 7524 2068 2
Charlton Athletic FC	David Ramzan	0 7524 1504 2
Crystal Palace FC	Revd Nigel Sands	0 7524 1544 1
Crewe Alexandra FC	Harold Finch	0 7524 1545 X
Crystal Palace FC	Nigel Sands	0 7524 1544 1
Gillingham FC	Roger Triggs	0 7524 2063 1
Grecian Voices	Dave Fisher/Gerald Gosling	0 7524 1621 9
Hull City FC	Chris Elton	0 7524 1620 0
Ipswich Town FC	Tony Garnett	0 7524 2152 2
Leeds United FC	David Saffer/Howard Dapin	0 7524 1642 1
Leeds United in Europe	David Saffer/Howard Dapin	0 7524 2043 7
Manchester City FC	David Saffer	0 7524 2085 2
Merthyr Tydfil FC	David Watkins	0 7524 1813 0
Millwall FC 1885-1939	Millwall FC Museum	0 7524 1849 1
Northampton Town FC	David Walden/John Watson	0 7524 1671 5
Oxford United FC	Jon Murray	0 7524 1183 7
Plymouth Argyle FC	Gordon Sparks	0 7524 1185 3
Queens Park Rangers FC	Tony Williamson	0 7524 1604 9
Reading FC: 1871-1997	David Downs	0 7524 1061 X
Rotherham United FC	Gerry Somerton	0 7524 1670 7
Southend United FC	David Goody/Peter Miles	0 7524 2089 5
Swindon Town FC	Richard Mattick	0 7524 2093 3
Tottenham Hotspur FC	Roy Brazier	0 7524 2044 5
Vetch Field Voices	Keith Haynes/Phil Sumbler	0 7524 1592 1
Walsall FC	Geoff Allman	0 7524 2091 7
West Brom FC	Tony Matthews	0 7524 2056 9
Wrexham FC	Gareth Davies/Peter Jones	0 7524 1899 8
York City FC	David Batters	0 7524 1568 9

Contents

Introduction		7
1.	The Preparations	9
2.	Games before the Final	34
3.	The Final	84
4.	Aftermath	126
Appendices		137

Also by Norman Shiel, this is a fascinating illustrated history of the FA Cup finals between the wars. It contains rare action shots, team photographs, programme covers and other items of memorabilia.

128 pages, 215 illustrations (b/w)
ISBN 0 7524 1669 3
£9.99

A beautifully written and lavishly illustrated history of the national side. Covering the team's history from the gentlemen of England in the nineteenth century to the last match at Wembley at the beginning of the twenty-first, this is an essential read for anyone with an interest in the history of football.

224 pages, 210 illustrations (colour and b/w)
0 7524 2042 9
£17.99

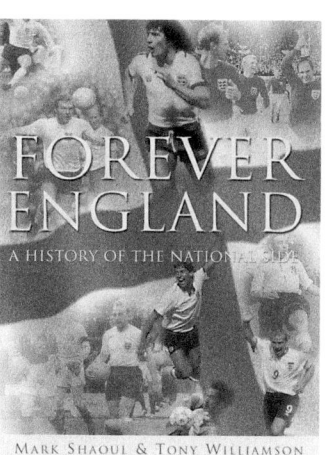

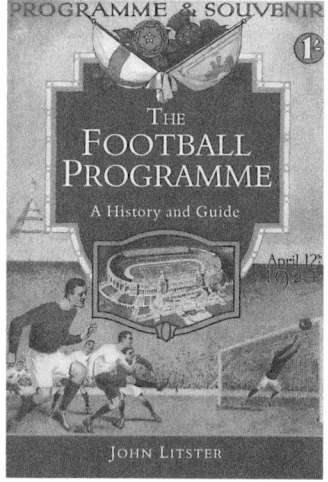

A detailed history and collectors' guide to the football programme. Written by John Litster, an acknowledged expert on these evocative artefacts, it contains many illustrations of the most significant and unusual examples.

172 pages, 150 illustrations (colour and b/w)
0 7524 1855 6
£12.99

The Jules Rimet Cup being handed back to Sir Stanley Rous, president of FIFA, at the conclusion of the draw for the 1966 World Cup finals.

Introduction

'There had never been a day like it in the history of English football and there can not be another like it at Wembley until England's turn comes round again to stage the World Cup, and the stadium is chosen for the second time as the venue of the greatest of soccer finals. That, if the members of FIFA exert their rights, is unlikely to happen until the year 2000 has long been gone and forgotten.'

This was written in 1972 by Harry Gee in his book on the first fifty years of Wembley. We are now at the Millennium and the prospect of another World Cup final at Wembley is not as remote as it seemed then. It will, however, not be the Wembley that Gee was writing about nor will it be very much like the summer of 1966.

Comparisons are all too often invidious and invariably subjective. No one can dispute, however, that 1966 was very special. It remains for a great many individuals, myself included, a real high point in their lives. It was a different world then, yet it comes to life through the collective memories of those who were there. It is not about exclusivity, though there is no little pride in being able to say of the final 'I was there', but about sharing. Those of us who were then teenagers are now getting on and those who were old enough to be involved directly are a rapidly dwindling band.

If anyone just wants to know the statistics then these have been published many times and are included in this book in summary form. If anyone just wants to see the game then the video of the whole final is readily available. If, however, you want to feel something of what it was really like as a player, official, administrator and, most of all, supporter, then these memories go a long way towards making that possible. What was it like to get tickets for such a major event? Tickets were printed before, at least in some cases, final capacities had been decided. Some made money by selling tickets at inflated prices; others had tickets given to them free by strangers. What was it like to meet, mingle with, and become, in some cases, lifelong friends with overseas fans? What was it like to have had your wedding or your confirmation service scheduled for the afternoon of 30 July only to find the vicar and bishops, respectively, more interested in events elsewhere. There was almost no violence or aggression, yet a senior FIFA official ended up with a half orange squashed into his face. There was almost no incursions onto the pitch yet a full scale match took place on the same energy-sapping Wembley turf the day after England's glorious victory. There were those who left Wembley after ninety minutes to catch their trains and thus missed out on the drama of extra time; and even those who came to meet friends and walked in free for that very drama.

When stated as facts these can only go so far. The global picture of life, attitudes and experiences from what would have been a wonderful time even without the World Cup, comes from the full range of the memories recorded here. Inevitably, given the numbers involved, there are far more left out than included, and I will always be very pleased to hear from anyone else who would like to share with me their own personal memories of 1966. Meanwhile, I hope that those of you who were there will enjoy reliving some of the magic through the memories recorded here, and those who are too young to have been there will get some idea of just what made it all so magical for those who were.

I am much indebted to all those clubs who kindly allowed me a little space in their programmes and greatly enjoyed hearing from fans of all those clubs. Thanks also to the AFS, the various county associations, and especially to the World Cup (1966) Association, whose members have kept alive that great spirit which this book seeks to capture. Thanks most especially to all those who were so willing to share their memories and make this book possible, and finally, thanks to my family for their patience and George in particular for his skills on the keyboard.

Norman Shiel
September 2000

CHAPTER 1
The Preparations

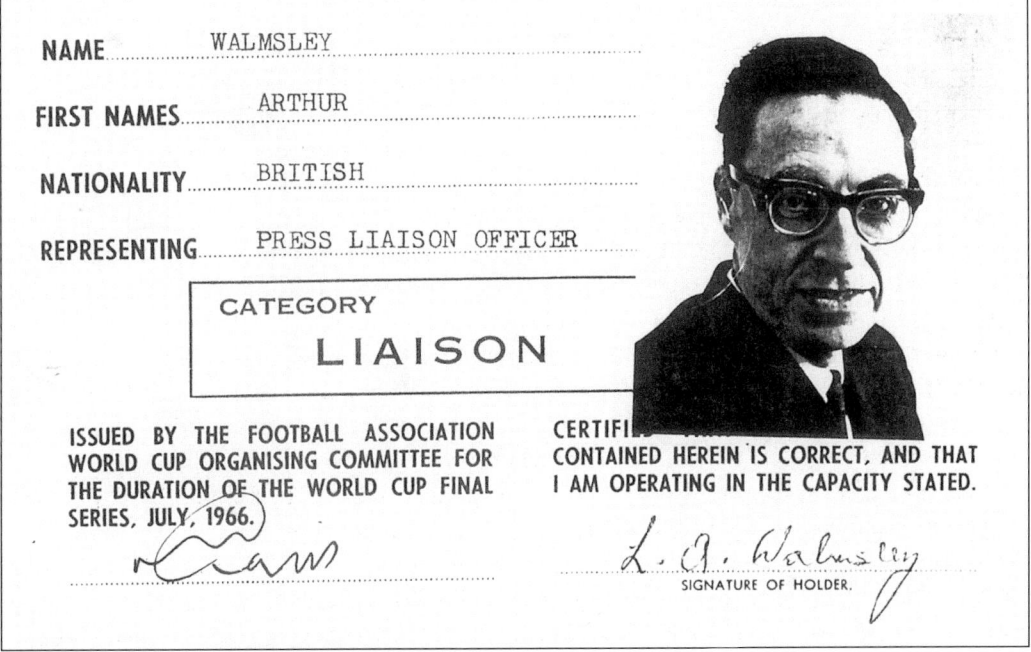

An official pass for the 1966 World Cup finals.

Press Liason Officer

I was a close friend of Mat Busby and it was he who asked me to get involved, some two years before the actual games, with the Manchester World Cup Organising Committee. Even though my health was not at its best that was very much the sort of offer that you just couldn't refuse. We were lucky in having such a wonderful chairman of our committee in Jim Buckley. He was the secretary of the National Federation of Boys Clubs and a superb organiser. He also had that wonderful gift of diplomacy whereby he could defuse any crisis and smooth out any conflict that might arise. All this ensured that we had a smooth trouble-free run in to the games even though it was a hell of a big operation setting it all up.

My own job was to set up two press centres, one at the ground for use by the media actually on match days; and another in

Letters concerning the arrangements.

Letters of appreciation.

A plan of Old Trafford showing the area allocated to the press contingent.

the city for all their other work. This one had to be more of a social centre as well, with catering and so forth, and we were allowed the use of the Renold Building, now part of Manchester Tech. Everyone right across the board was so helpful and co-operative: the Post Office, the Corporation, the police, and the club. At the dinner held afterwards, one of the Post Office representatives said that it had been such a successful example of teamwork that it was a pity not to keep it all going and was there not something else that could be organised along such lines again. We received special commendations from both home and abroad and Frank McGhee said that the arrangements were the best that he had experienced anywhere.

I went to the games at Old Trafford. We were all disappointed that we did not get the Brazilians in Manchester. The actual games were themselves not very memorable in the end and the crowds adequate but nothing very special.

One little incident I remember was when I heard a kafuffle at an entrance at one end of Old Trafford. It was Bill Shankly trying to get in to do some reporting which he had been commissioned to do. He had been given a stand ticket but no press pass and was being refused entry by the man at the press entrance and was not at all pleased by this saying in no uncertain terms that this was not the sort of welcome he was used to at Old Trafford. I got him in and gave the stand ticket to someone else.

Arthur Walmsley

Commentator

As BBC anchorman I had been commentating since 1948 and got on well with the players, although in those days players tended to be fairly wary of the media for the most part. I was commentator in 1966 for about fifteen games. Of course the World Cup in 1966 was quite a low-key event. It was well organised but even so there were problems over ticket allocations.

Wembley was a wonderful place to have such a stadium – in 1923! In the World Cup year the FA made a profit but instead of sharing it out amongst the county associations they kept it and lost most of it to the government. There wasn't much commercialism then and it was a great honour to play for your country in those days. You certainly didn't get much money for it.

The players were very close. That's why we won – they were at ease. As for Alf, he is the only one who has won anything. He didn't suffer fools gladly. All the players thought the world of him.

There were no problems with the media as far as I can recall. We could have had colour but the government wouldn't allow it. We were very annoyed. The BBC were

The commentary team, from left to right: Wolstenholme, Barnes, Coleman, Bough and Weekes.

geared up for it. This meant that Mexico were first with colour in 1970.

On the day of the final we had a 9.00 a.m. start and got ready for a long day ahead. The BBC people helped a lot of other countries. In those days the cameras were cumbersome things – I well remember how difficult it was getting one in position at the most hair-raising of sites on top of the clock stand at Roker Park. There were, however, nothing like so many in use at a game as there are now. Everything went off very well.

Interviews were done afterwards but it was nothing like what players have to put up with nowadays. The lads then set off on a slow journey to the hotel. I left about 7.00 p.m. and was very tired so I went home and went to bed.

It was a football match rather than a spectacle. It was just left to the players to entertain.

Kenneth Wolstenholme

Merchandising Man

In 1965 the Sunderland Supporters Association was formed and because I had managed to sell two gross of pens I was appointed sales manager, with no other previous experience!

In the run-up to the World Cup we decided to buy a large quantity of corncrakes which had been offered to us by Fulham FC. They were ex-war department items on offer at about a pound each I think. They were brought back from Fulham in the boot of the Supporters Club bus towards the end of the 1965/66 season.

When we saw them, for the first time, they were covered in grease and stank of creosote. We had them taken to my house where friends and I worked hard to clean them all up then paint them. They had a galvanised metal plate down one side and were very stiff, probably requiring two hands to work them. They wouldn't be allowed now.

We decided to paint them up to appeal to the visiting fans, especially the Italians, so we painted colours and even individual players' names such as Mazzola on. Then we took them all to Roker Park to sell. The visiting fans were not really interested in having their team colours or players on but wanted 'Willie'! We thus had to get World Cup Willie stickers and then we were able to sell them all, but our time and handiwork with the paintbrushes was largely wasted.

We had a request from the Russian delegation that was staying locally to take some souvenirs to where they were staying. They had hardly any sterling at all, something like £8 for all of them for the whole stay. They flocked round our tables of souvenirs but wanted to barter rather than buy. They had brought with them loads of badges and similar souvenirs relating to Russian spacemen and Russian sport in general. In the end we got used to doing it all through barter and only took 2s 3d in actual money!

Another group wanted us to go up to their room with the souvenirs; a big wrestler was especially taken by some retractable pens we had and which we had been selling for a shilling. He wanted them all but for exchanges with other badges, caviar and even bottles of vodka. I teased him when I found out that the reason he was so keen on the pens was that they cost a whole rouble each in Russia, and said he was a capitalist. He seemed outraged but another of the Russians – whom we nicknamed 'The

Clown' because he was always joking – saw it as very funny.

A little Mongolian guy tried to get us to buy all his Russian money from him as a way of getting some sterling. I was very wary of the notes in case they were fakes so we stayed well clear of those although we might have been able to make a tidy profit on them if we had taken a chance. As it was we ended up with a large quantity of Russian coinage.

We left after that 'sales trip' with loads of Russian badges of various sorts, quite a lot of Russian money in coins but not notes, and just 2s 3d in English money. When I found out that neither bank nor travel agent would exchange the Russian coinage I was worried about being stuck with it and making a loss. In the end we had some cards printed with the Sunderland Black Cat on the cover and Russian coins of different denominations stuck on and then sold them all as souvenirs! All the badges also sold so we ended up doing very well.

The preparations for and activity during the 1966 World Cup really set the Supporters Club on a sound footing and we have been going ever since. Everything was done on a voluntary basis and I remember we had a super sales team of volunteers that pulled together and made everything work.

G. Forster

Match Liaison Officer

I was a match liaison officer. The FA operation was based at the White City and as the date for the actual finals got nearer the

The England team at their hotel.

The arrangements for meeting the various overseas parties as they arrived in Britain.

WORLD CUP 1966
COMPETING TEAMS - ARRIVAL OF OFFICIAL PARTIES
(as notified up to 6th June, 1966).

COUNTRY	AIRPORT	DATE	TIME	FLIGHT NO.	
France	London	8 July	17.40	BE.5399 From Edinburgh.	
Mexico	London	3 July	21.25	Alitalia 300 From Rome.	
Uruguay	London	1 July*	04/5	from Barcelona	
Argentina	London	2 or 3 July*	To be advised.	To be advised	
West Germany	Manchester	8 July	19.25	BE.4116	
Spain	London	7 July	16.45	BE.049	
Switzerland	Castle Donnington	8 July	21.50	Balair Charter Kloten.	
Brazil	Manchester	7 July	14.10	BE.853 From Copenhagen.	
Bulgaria	London	4 July	(19.45)	LZ.129 — 22.05 PM IN M/C	
Hungary	Manchester	4 July	10.05	KLM.149	
Portugal	Manchester	8 July	14.10	AF.960	
Chile		7 July	To be advised.	To be advised.	
Italy	London)	7 July	14.50	BE.743 From Copenhagen.	
	Newcastle)	7 July	18.30	BKS.456 From London.	
Korea	-	30 June	-	Via Berlin.	
U.S.S.R.	London	6 July	To be advised.	From Goteborg.	

Note: * indicates - Verbal Only

FA realised that there was a need for extra liaison staff to meet the visiting teams and just to make it all actually work. I was then assistant secretary at Spurs and when the club was asked if they would make someone available it fell to me.

This work came on stream from about March 1966. I teamed up with Leslie Taylor of Middlesex Wanderers who was an expert in travel arrangements. We took one team each from those in the London group. At the White City the pitch was only just big enough. Extra turf had to be put in at the last minute to fit the corner kicks in properly. I was in overall charge for that game at the White City but it was a poor game on the night.

I remember going to the airport at about 4.00 a.m. to meet the party from Uruguay.

Another of our roles was to supervise the random drugs tests. I ended up in charge of the Argentine team on the occasion of their quarter-final game with England. There was no way they were going to allow anyone access to their dressing rooms that day! When the names were drawn for which players should be tested it just had to be Ratin's name that came out. He absolutely refused so the medics just gave up on it. It simply couldn't happen like that now.

When it came to the final Leslie Taylor took Germany and I took England. I knew Alf a little through Spurs. I didn't have to do a very great deal because the pattern was by that stage pretty well established.

It was wonderful to be at the heart of it all, just a few seats behind Ramsey. I began

15

to worry about the apparent lack of security after the game as regards the trophy itself. We agreed that we should shadow it given that it had already been stolen once! In those days the stewards were rather ancient. It eventually got back to the dressing room. I went into the dressing room and drank champagne out of the cup – in small quantities because the top was so small!

At one stage everyone was looking around on the dressing room floor for Nobby Stiles contact lens.

I then travelled back with the team on the bus to the Hendon Hall Hotel for a champagne reception. I can recall Bobby Charlton in the middle of the room weeping with emotion. His big brother, Jack, was the opposite – totally laid back about it all.

All the way back from the hotel to the Royal Garden was absolute pandemonium with cheering crowds and hooting horns.

I recall Harold Wilson and his drunken sidekick George Brown milking it for all it was worth. I cannot remember how or when I got home after that!

In my view the performance of the day on a very heavy pitch was that of Alan Ball who ran everywhere.

Alan Leather

Travel Agent

I was employed at the time as a travel consultant with Thomas Cook and Son, as they were then known, dealing with in-coming visitors who had booked their travel arrangements in our overseas offices. A couple of my colleagues, including Cyril Broderick, were seconded to the match ticket centre, which was set up in our Berkeley Street office.

Ours was always a very busy office but the high spot was immediately following the exit of Brazil from the competition. We were inundated with Brazilians wanting to return home as they had no further interest. Unfortunately for them, they were all travelling on air tickets which allowed no changes from the dates of travel shown and were not endorsable to another airline or refundable. In other words they were stuck here until the date they were due to travel, which I think was the best part of another two weeks.

Many of them bought new one-way tickets home which cost more than their original returns and others booked on package tours or coach tours to the continent rather than hang around London in their misery. I know Cooks made a lot of money and I worked on commission at that time!

Some airlines had organised hospitality visits to Wembley for groups of travel agents and I saw two matches this way. I think they were a boring 0-0 draw with Uruguay and I believe France were involved in the other game but can't be sure. These visits were nothing like the lavish corporate entertainment provided today – just a few beers and a sandwich and a coach to the game.

On the Friday evening before leaving the office the ticket centre was offering tickets for the final and I picked one up for a couple of pounds. Imagine my feelings when I took up my place behind the far goal from the tunnel in a sea of red, yellow and black flags. My so-called friends hadn't told me the ticket was from German allocation, but that was in the days when there was no hassle and I escaped unscathed.

Geoff Marsh

'Queen'

I was given the job of playing the role of the Queen for the dress rehearsal of the opening ceremony so that all the arrangements and the timings could be checked out. My boss was to play Prince Philip. We ran through it but despite our best efforts to go slowly we were told to do it again because it was too fast.

I was then told to say something for a sound test which I thought was a bit pointless in an empty stadium but I started off with, 'My husband and I...'

On the day of the final I saw hardly any of the game because I was in an office in the stadium with two CID officers responsible for the security of the trophy. I only left it for an extended toilet break when I managed to see just a little of the game live. Otherwise the whole time was spent in the office with the trophy watching the game on TV.

Mrs Ellis

Referees' Liaison Officer

I was in charge of all the match officials having officiated myself at the previous finals in Chile. All the officials were based in London at the Kensington Close Hotel. In the hotel I set up an office, room 104, for all thirty-two officials. There was plenty to do.

The North Korean referee Choi had with him an equally short and slight compatriot as interpreter. Adidas had been

The programme of events for the opening ceremony.

THE OPENING CEREMONY

6 p.m.
Programme of Music
by the Massed Bands of the Grenadier Guards, the Coldstream Guards, and the Irish Guards.

6.40 p.m.
Marching Display
by the Massed Bands of the Brigade of Guards: the Grenadier Guards, Coldstream Guards, Irish Guards, Scots Guards, and the Welsh Guards.

7.05 p.m.
Flag bearing ceremony of the competing nations.

7.15 p.m.
Her Majesty the Queen
accompanied by His Royal Highness, The Duke of Edinburgh, arrives on the arena.

Fanfare of Trumpets.

National Anthem.

Her Majesty is invited by Sir Stanley Rous, President of the F.I.F.A., to open the Final Series of the Eighth World Championship.

Her Majesty declares the Championship open.

Raising of flags of competing nations.

Teams enter the arena.

Presentation of Officials to Her Majesty.

Uruguayan National Anthem.

Teams presented to Her Majesty.

7.30 p.m.
KICK-OFF.   ENGLAND v URUGUAY.

Left: *The order of events.* Right: *Her Majesty the Queen greets Bobby Moore.*

Queen Elizabeth II opens the 1966 World Cup finals at Wembley.

The parade of the finalists' flags at the opening ceremony.

supplied with sizes for all the kit and shortly after it had been issued referee Choi and his interpreter came to the office. Choi through the interpreter said that the boots were much too big. I said 'tell him to put them on'. They clearly were far too big and made him look like Donald Duck. I said that the problem really was that his feet were too small. What had in fact happened was that size two had been written as one-one and thus taken as eleven.

On the first night there was a dinner at the Guildhall and all the referees met the Prime Minister Harold Wilson. From the referees' point of view never before or since have they been entertained as they were in 1966. A programme was arranged for every day with several alternative options for them to sign up for or not as they chose. In the evening were theatre visits or musicals. During the day sailing, lunch with the Marquis of Bath at Longleat, tours of all the major sights, museums and galleries, RAC club, Ascot, river trips and so on.

The fourth official was introduced for the first time in 1966. I did the appointments for the final round, based on all the permutations of nationality, language, politics and so on. Whilst doing this I said to my wife, 'Here am I struggling with all this. What if someone pulls a muscle and can't carry on?' Concern about this led to local officials being briefed and on standby in case of emergency; a fourth official.

One month before the opening game I was sent twenty footballs. There was no mention of the pressure in the laws then. I blew them all up and tested them with my pupils on the school field. All the balls had dropped in pressure because they had increased in size. I therefore decided that an official pressure should be clearly laid down.

REFEREES FOR THE TOURNAMENT

Referees who will have charge of matches in the Final Series were chosen in Barcelona at a meeting of the FIFA Referees' Committee. There were 148 nominations from 82 FIFA member associations.

Fourteen African nations submitted the names of 24 referees; from 17 Asian associations 25 names were put forward; 31 European associations made 62 nominations; 12 North Central American and Caribbean associations recommended 22 officials; and the remaining 15 were listed by South American countries.

The principle of selecting seven referees from the organising country, and one from each competing finalist country, was maintained. It was decided to select a further nine referees from countries whose teams do not appear in the last 16.

The designation of referees and linesmen for duty at the 32 games in the Final Series, and other decisions relating to refereeing during the tournament, will be taken by Sir Stanley Rous, President of FIFA, and the following members of the Referees' Committee: Dr. M. Andrejevic (Yugoslavia), Mr. P. Escartin (Spain), Mr. N. Latyshev (U.S.S.R.), Mr. A. Lindenberg (Switzerland) and Mr. Koe Ewe Teik (Malaysia).

All the referees and linesmen will be chosen from this list:

Competing Countries

Argentine	ROBERTO GOICOECHEA	Brazil	ARMANDO MARQUES
Bulgaria	DIMITER ROUMENTCHEV	Chile	CLAUDIO VICUNA
England	KEVIN HOWLEY	England	JAMES FINNEY
England	WILLIAM CLEMENTS	England	ERNEST CRAWFORD
England	KENNETH DAGNALL	England	GEORGE McCABE
England	JOHN TAYLOR	France	PIERRE SCHWINTE
West Germany	RUDOLF KREITLEIN	Hungary	ISTVAN ZSOLT
Italy	CONCETTO LO BELLO	North Korea	CHOI DUK RYONG
Mexico	FERNANDO BUERGO ELCUAZ	Portugal	JOAQUIM FERNANDES CAMPOS
Spain	JUAN GARDEAZABAL	Switzerland	GOTTFRIED DIENST
U.S.S.R.	TOFIK BAKHRAMOV	Uruguay	JOSE MARIA CODESAL

Non-Finalist Countries

Czechoslovakia	Dr. KAROI GALBA	Northern Ireland	JOHN ADAIR
Israel	MENACHEM ASHKENASI	Peru	ARTURO YAMASAKI
Scotland	HUGH PHILLIPS	Sweden	BERTIL LOOW
United Arab Republic	ALY KANDIL	Wales	LEO CALLAGHAN
	Yugoslavia	KONSTANTIN ZECEVIC	

Reserves: KURT TSCHENSCHER (West Germany) and H. M. ANGULLIA (Singapore)

Left: *Harry Cavan, FIFA official.* Right: *The list of referees for the tournament.*

Sir Stanley Rous, the president of FIFA, selects balls for use in the finals

Referee Kreitlein is escorted from the field after the England v. Argentina game, in which he sent off Ratin.

In the event most of the balls used ended the games verging on illegality in terms of size and most were re-inflated at half time.

The introduction of red and yellow cards came as a direct result of the England v. Argentina game. Kreitlein the referee had no language in common with the players of either side. He sent off Ratin who was reluctant to go. I decided to get involved in case the game should have to be abandoned and I persuaded Ratin to leave the field by a combination of broken Spanish and gestures. Ratin wanted an interpreter.

The Charlton brothers were cautioned in this game and did not realise it. Ramsay was unaware of it. It was confirmed in the referee's report. While driving home afterwards I came to traffic lights at the junction with Kensington High Street. Waiting at the lights I got the idea of colour coding from yellow for caution and red for stop. The coloured cards were introduced for the next World Cup. They were always meant to address the problems of language and were always intended to be the confirmation of a caution rather than a replacement for it.

At the end of the Argentine game the referee was a long way from the tunnel when he blew and it was no easy business getting him off safely. When the Argentine players came off they were given their half oranges as usual. In the tunnel some players were kicking at the panels of the England team coach. Harry Cavan (senior FIFA official) went up to remonstrate with them and got half an orange shoved in his face. He said while cleaning his glasses, 'And I've got to go into their dressing room for a doping sample!' Some of the other Argentine players were kicking at the door of the England dressing room.

In the England dressing room just before the final, three drug testers came in carrying aloft a chamber pot on which was the World Cup logo and, in letraset, 'World Cup Piddling Champion! Jack Charlton, three times' – his name had been drawn for testing on three occasions!

Tofik Bakhramov was not very well placed to make a decision about the controversial goal being about fifteen yards up from the corner flag. Experience teaches you how much daylight you have to see in order to allow a goal. Bakhramov later said it was not a goal but the referee had already committed himself so he merely agreed.

Ken Aston

Chauffeur

I was a long distance lorry driver in 1966 and got the job of being the chauffeur for the North Korean party during its stay in the North East. This came about through Harry Green the secretary to Middlesbrough. I did the work during my two weeks annual leave plus one week's leave of absence. I got paid directly by FIFA and can't remember the exact figure but it

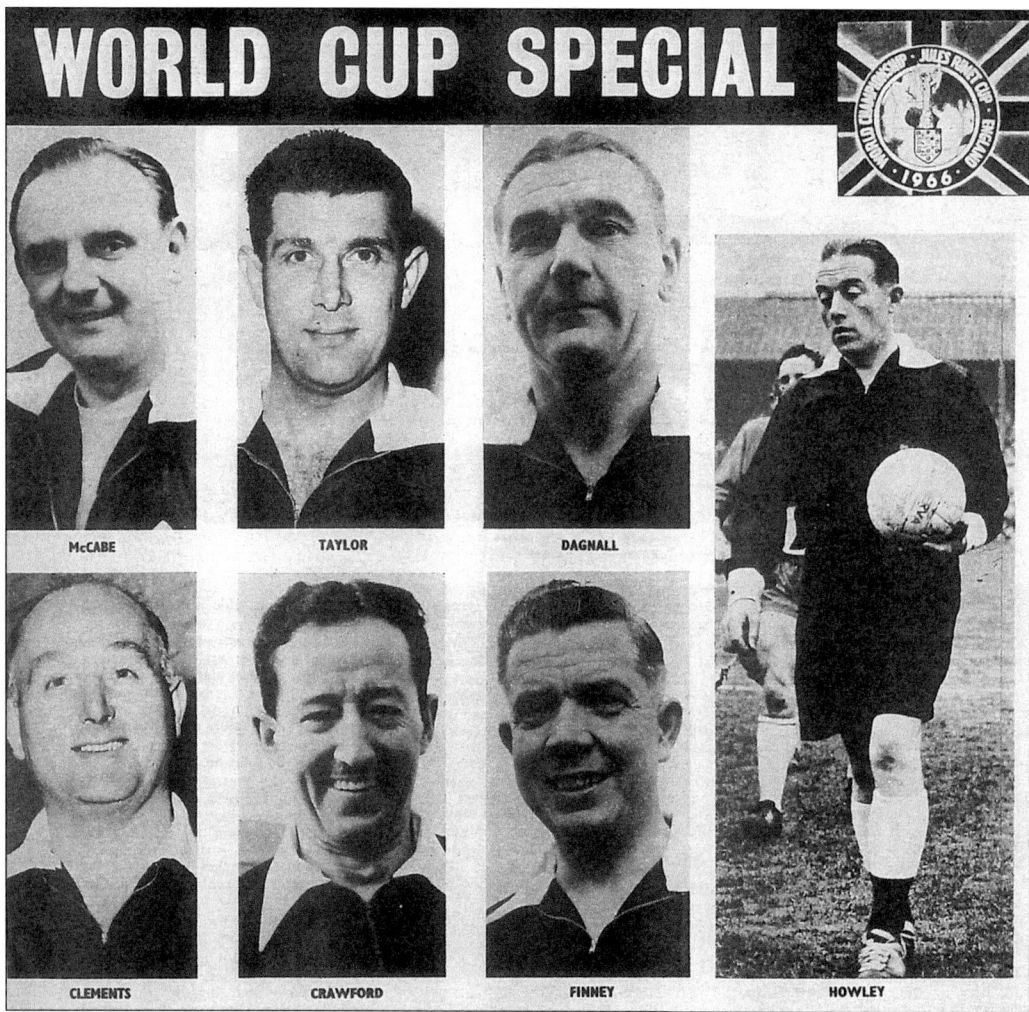

The British referees who officiated in the 1966 World Cup finals.

260

To mark the concluding stages of the 1966 Association Football World Cup Competition (The Jules Rimet Cup)

The Prime Minister

requests the honour of the company of

Mr. and Mrs. G. C. Burrell

at Dinner in Guildhall, on Saturday, 9th July, 1966 at 6.30 p.m. for 7.30 p.m.

Black Tie or Lounge Suit   *Please reply to: The Secretary, Government Hospitality, 72, Whitehall, s.w.1*
Telephone: Whi 1481 Ext. 402

An invitation to the Prime Minister's dinner to mark the concluding stages of the 1966 World Cup.

was about £150 altogether.

The Koreans were staying at the Middleton St George Hotel near the airport. Every morning we went out there for 9.00 a.m. and were then at their disposal. Altogether there were three big limousines but I did more driving than the others and got on best with the interpreters. The players trained every morning and they ate lots of chocolate and were very keen on old comedy films like Charlie Chaplin and Popeye.

One day an interpreter came to say that a player had spilled something on his suit and could they go to a chemist to buy something to get the stains out. I took him into Middlesbrough in the big black limousine with the North Korean flag flying. They insisted that the word North was not used and that they were just Koreans. As soon as the car stopped at the chemists a crowd gathered. We got the stain remover and it worked so well that I had to take him back to get the entire stock in case it happened again.

I took them to Lloyds bank where they drew out loads of money. Another trip was to the Cleveland centre to record interviews with local people about the visitors so they could be used on Korean radio. The locals were asked questions for use in the broadcasts.

One day when the party was out sightseeing in Middlesbrough they saw the flags on top of the Town Hall and wanted to film them close up. I wondered how to achieve this and decided to approach the manager of the Odeon cinema. After the situation was explained to him he let the Koreans out on his roof so they could film the flags and indeed the whole Middlesbrough skyline.

We went to a mayor's banquet at Sunderland. I had to take around all the tickets, which had been dished out by Harry Green to all four participating countries. The Italians and Chileans were no bother but at the agricultural college in Durham I encountered two 'KGB' giants on the gate who simply would not let me in. I just gave all the tickets to them and left.

For the actual banquet I took the president of the Korean FA and all the interpreters and coaches. They had become increasingly friendly as time went on so I was invited into the banquet itself. A commissionaire tried to stop them but the Korean attitude was 'No driver; no Koreans', a stand taken by their president and communicated by their interpreters. I was the only driver to get in and I ended up sitting on a round table with the Korean president, Lev Yashin, and Jack Taylor among others. After the meal the Mayoress of Sunderland came over to get her menu card signed and so I made up some imaginary Korean characters and she went away happy.

There was a different level of hospitality and friendliness between Middlesbrough and Sunderland. At Ayresome Park Harry Green gave out tickets to all the drivers who had brought teams or dignitaries to the games and there was somewhere convenient for them to park and a voucher for a buffet meal. They were put in what was an old press box. At Sunderland we took the president of the Korean FA to the game between Chile and Russia and drove right to the very doors of Roker Park, waved through by the police. When I asked where to park however, I was told, 'You don't park anywhere near here!' I had to go miles away back over the bridge and park and walk all the way back. When I got there and asked for a ticket I was told, 'No tickets for you lot here!' By chance Stan Anderson happened to be passing and he had two spares in his pocket, so I and one other got in.

I took the Korean coaches to Liverpool to see Portugal play Brazil on the same night as Korea played Italy. I got a super seat in the grandstand and watched the game while the coaches made their notes. Afterwards they were desperate to know how Korea had done so we used a call box and rang the social club in Middlesbrough to learn of the 1-0 victory. The coaches were dancing about on the pavement at that.

I was then invited to the quarter-final at Goodison Park with the official Korean party. I stayed with the players, had lunch with them and then a seat at the game. If they had won then I'd have gone all the way with them.

Mr Swailes

Player

Alf had us believing we could win it and he himself certainly believed we could do it but I think he made his public statement that we would win rather tongue in cheek and then ended up stuck with it.

The first game was disappointing but things gradually improved as the tournament progressed. The great expectation at the start was dampened by the opening game in which Uruguay were intent on playing for a draw. Once we'd won the group however, things began to take off.

I have a clear memory of Ratin being ordered off and refusing to go and everyone waiting for what seemed like ages before he eventually did. The other players were stood around chatting then all of a sudden a great cheer went up. It was because it had been announced that North Korea were beating Portugal 3-0. I remember thinking that that game looked set to provide the shock result of the tournament. At the end of the Argentine game there was no blanket instruction about shirts, just Alf stopping George Cohen because he was so upset by the Argentinian behaviour. There was no banquet or fraternising anyway after any of the games until the final itself.

R. Hunt   Roger Hunt.

Wembley Press box view of Roger Hunt's first goal for England in the group match against France.

Hunt scores for England.

25

Another goal for Hunt, this time against France.

The Girlfriend

I didn't go to all the games. Before the final Kay Stiles, John Connelly's wife and I went shopping and bought ourselves new outfits. Mine was a red, white and blue combination.

The lads were not staying with us. At the final I sat with Alan's mum and all the wives. When we were 2-1 up and there was only a few minutes to go the squad players were all asked to go down. I fainted for the first and, so far, the only time in my life when Germany scored their equaliser. It was as though the whole atmosphere had been sucked out of the stadium. All the squad players then made their way back.

All the wives went back to the Royal Garden Hotel but were not allowed into the official reception. Afterwards everybody was going on to the Playboy Club. We met up outside the club but they wanted us to go in all at once and we were corralled outside until everyone was there. A group of us decided to go to Danny La Rue's – Nobby and his wife, John Connelly and Geoff Hurst and their wives and us. There we were treated like kings. They didn't know we were coming but within an hour they had produced a special cake modelled on the World Cup.

Next day after the match the players went to the BBC for a luncheon and interview. They got more money for their BBC appearances than for winning the World Cup! The win bonus for the World Cup was £1,000, taxed. After that interview we went home with Nobby and Kay Stiles and on the way we stopped off at Knutsford Services for egg and chips and a look at the medals. Imagine doing that now!

Mrs L. Ball

Steward

I was a steward at the 1966 World Cup final. I had just qualified as a referee and was only eighteen at the time. I saw an advert in the local referees' magazine asking for stewards for the games at Wembley. I applied to be a steward at all nine games but never really thought I'd be accepted. In fact

I was accepted for all nine.

Once our job was done we were allowed to find empty seats and sit in them. My best views were for the quarter-final and then the final itself, where I was virtually on the halfway line just opposite the Royal Box.

My best memory of the semi-final was of being on the pitch two hours before the game when the Portuguese players were getting familiar with the place. I was able to get nearly all their autographs, including Eusebio.

I was a police cadet at the time and in order to do the stewarding I took my two weeks holiday which covered most of the games and was allowed extra leave for the other two games because my boss felt it was experience relevant to my training.

I went up by train from Brighton each day. We had to be there four hours before the game. We got no travel money or pay but we got a sandwich voucher so we could have something to eat during our shift, and our steward's badge. I was told by a permanent steward that if I hung on to my badge and showed it on future occasions at Wembley they would let me in. I never had the bottle to try it. I still have the badge and the special tickets we got as stewards.

Graham Tate

Steward 2

By virtue of being a council member of the Oxfordshire FA, I attended all the games at Wembley as a steward.

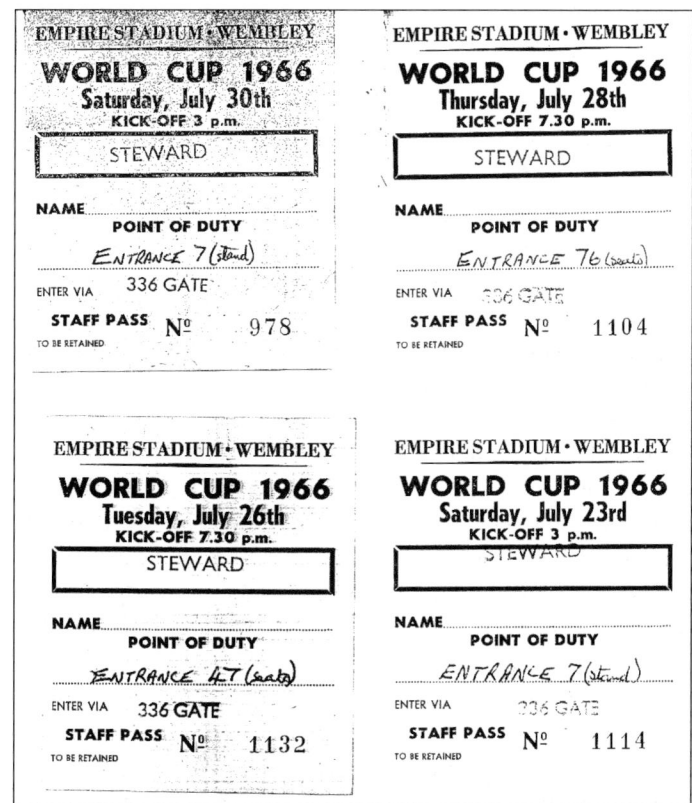

Stewards' passes for some of the games held at Wembley.

An enamelled Wembley steward's badge from the 1966 finals.

We had to report an hour before the game; were issued with a steward's badge and a voucher to obtain a sandwich and a cup of tea before going to the allotted berth ready for 1.00 p.m. when the public were admitted.

The nightmare was being a steward – unpaid of course – in the standing enclosures or pens. You were instructed to keep the grockles as near to the front as possible. You can imagine someone after three or four pints saying 'I've paid my money for a ticket and I can stand where I bloody well like.'

At kick-off there was scarcely room to move and inevitably at half time the call of nature made it virtually impossible to get to a toilet so it was a case of watch out chum.

Thank goodness I had a seating enclosure for the final and I have two abiding memories from that. An English-speaking German offered me five five pound notes (£25) for my steward's badge. After I refused he asked me, for some obscure reason, to autograph his programme and of course I gladly complied. The other abiding memory which will live for all time is of the almost toothless Nobby Stiles dancing round the pitch with the trophy. What a happy day!

J. Roughton

Ball Boy

I had previously been a ball boy at the England *v.* Scotland game in 1965. Bedfordshire was chosen to provide ball boys for the World Cup and my name came out of the hat. I was a ball boy at the other end from where the controversial goal was scored. We were shown round Wembley, including the dressing rooms. I was at the end opposite the tunnel with one other. We were instructed to roll the ball back and not try to kick it. The ball boys went out first followed by the players. Afterwards we ran into the middle. We got to keep the basic kit but not the tracksuits. I was recently invited to appear on the *Big Breakfast* show because of my 'famous memories'.

R. Jones

Casual

In the sixties there was a crew of workers at Wembley, called the casuals, who all had other jobs but who lived nearby and could therefore come in on a casual basis for clearing up after big events like cup finals and so on. My dad was one of these while being a lorry driver. With the World Cup coming along they needed to recruit another force because of all the extra work and needed some workers who did not have other jobs so this basically became the student crew. I had just left school – and indeed left school a shade early – in order to do this particular job. The pay was wonderful but the work was very demanding I was able to make something like £30 a week at a time, when I could get just £5 a week for starting in a normal job. Best of all, however, were the perks, being able to get into any game or event free.

We used to sit together in the old tunnel at the opposite end of the ground to the main players' tunnel, where equipment and such like was stored.

On the day after the World Cup Final we were in as usual at 8.00 a.m. for the clean up. After a couple of hours of hard work we were told to down tools and a little lorry turned up with beer and sandwiches for us as an extra thank you. Then we had a game of football out on the full pitch between the student crew and the casuals. It was like playing on a sponge. I was then playing football regularly to a good local standard but it nearly killed me playing on that pitch. I just wondered how they had managed to keep going for so long the previous day.

I recall that on the morning of the final the groundsman, Percy, had been interviewed and in his response to the comment, 'You've a big game on today', he said, 'Yes, but an even bigger one tomorrow!', meaning the students *v.* casuals.

The stadium authorities were normally quite ruthless about their work ethic because the work just had to be completed so it was all the more special to get this sort of gratitude and concession on that Sunday.

Out from the Wembley tunnel and off to the right was an area where grass was being grown so as to provide turf when replacement was needed. During the World Cup they had to re-turf the goal area because of the wear it was getting. This has all gone now because of the price of land. The sides of the ground always drained better, especially where the speedway caused the regular replacement of turf. Sometimes they used to paint the grass for effect if there were any patches going a bit brown.

During the World Cup they still ran the greyhounds when there was no clash and on those nights we were in from 10.00 p.m. until 2.00 a.m. to clear up. We sometimes had little knockabouts under lights in the early hours of the morning. Wembley was a very spooky place at that sort of time, especially for me when I got to clear the area under the terraces with a mechanical sweeper all on my own. There were secret tunnels between levels. After the final one of the jobs I got was to dispose of all the ticket stubs taken at the turnstiles. They filled a whole industrial skip. Often things were found while cleaning the terraces – jewellery, cameras and money, especially ten bob notes which looked rather like the match tickets.

S. Banks

Fan

I well remember the sheer excitement, long before 1966, when I realised that the World Cup would be coming to England and that I would be old enough to go to matches, certainly in my part of the world, the North East, and probably the finals in London. I had no memory of the 1958 World Cup and that in Chile had seemed incredibly distant in every sense of the word with poor and ill-timed radio coverage. I also recall thinking with some shock how pitifully small the crowds were for some of the games in Chile. Sure that that would not happen in England, I was determined to get in my application on the very first possible day for a ten-match ticket. Regardless of who was going to be in the final I had to be there or regret it for the rest of my life – after all it was only £4 1s for ten matches. My application was dated 29-6-65 and was duly acknowledged. By late August that same year my tickets arrived, or so I thought but it was just a fancy form confirming that I had duly been allocated the ten-match ticket I had applied for. I was application number 99. The actual tickets were not to be sent out until the following April.

The logistics became the next problem. For the games in the North East I would be

---

Dear Sir,

World Cup - 1966

Receipt of your Application Form dated 29-6-65 and money in respect of World Cup Match Tickets is acknowledged.

Owing to the large number of applications received, it will be some time before we are able to confirm your application and despatch a Receipt Voucher.

Yours faithfully,

E. K. WILLSON
Chief Administrative Officer.

A postcard acknowledging receipt of an application for tickets.

okay as I went to school in Newcastle and Sunderland was not too far. It was for me and for many a real blow when the games that were scheduled for Newcastle were switched to Middlesbrough. I knew little and certainly cared nothing at all for the politics that lay behind all this. Newcastle was a bigger ground in a bigger city, would have drawn bigger crowds and would have been much more convenient for me! In the event I persuaded a school friend who had a driving license – much rarer then – to drive me to Middlesbrough and then back to stay at his house after each of the games there. Sunderland was easy enough and all the arrangements worked out very well. I was rather disappointed at the crowds, having been in absolutely packed 'full houses' at all the North Eastern grounds I had hoped for

The application form for tickets.

Brochure giving details of games and tickets.

```
INFORMATION FOR TICKET PURCHASERS:
These notes are to be read together with the Ticket Sales Brochure.
1.  The only way in which you can ensure that you obtain a place at the
    Final is to purchase a 10-Match Season Ticket.
2.  Other than 10-Match Season Tickets, the following is the composition
    of the Season Tickets:-
    (a) 7-Match.   All The 6 Eighth-Finals and the Quarter-Final in any
                   one group;
    (b) 4-Match.   The 3 Eighth-Finals and the Quarter-Final at a ground
                   which stages a Quarter-Final; and
    (c) 3-Match.   The 3 Eighth-Finals at a ground which does not stage a
                   Quarter-Final.
    All holders of these three types of Season Ticket will be eligible to take
    part in a ballot for tickets for the Final.  It is not possible to purchase,
    for instance, 3-Match Season Tickets for the Final, 3rd/4th Place Final and
    a Semi-Final.
3.  After the draw in January, 1966, assigning four of the 16 victorious teams
    to each of the 4 Groups, then 4- and 3-Match Season Tickets may be available
    for purchase by overseas visitors.
4.  Season Tickets will continue to be sold until the demand for them wanes.
    It is anticipated that in March or April, 1966 it will be possible to
    purchase single tickets for most matches.
5.  No single tickets will be available for the Final and it is not likely that
    many single tickets will be available for the Semi-Finals.
6.  All applications for 10- and 7-Match Season Tickets should be sent to the
    World Cup Organisation.  Applications for 4- and 3-Match Season Tickets
    should be sent to the box offices of the grounds concerned.
7.  Applications from home purchasers will be accepted on one form for up to a
    total of ten Season Tickets.  Separate application forms must, however, be
    completed for each type of Season Ticket required.
8.  Applicants for 4- and 3-Match Season Tickets should clearly indicate their
    choice of Ground on their application form after the words "Group Area
    Preference".  Hence, a request for a 4-Match Season at Everton would appear
    on the application form under the heading "B. Group Area Preference" as
    "EVERTON".
9.  If an applicant wishes to see some games in more than one group and the
    Final, he should apply for a 10-Match Season Ticket for one Group and a
    7-, 4- or 3-Match Season Ticket for any other Group of Ground.
10. Applicants for seats will have a far greater chance of success if they
    apply for Grade 2 rather than Grade 1 seats.
11. Applications by persons who wish to sit together should be made on the
    same form
12. Applications by persons in this country for themselves and also on behalf
    of individuals from abroad will be treated as home applications.  This
    includes applications by business houses who are applying on behalf of their
    representatives or business associates from overseas but does not apply to
    agencies in this country acting on behalf of agencies overseas.
13. Tickets cannot be used as prizes in lotteries or competitions.
    Competitions include giving tickets away as rewards to salesmen in sales
    promotion campaigns and/or prizes to consumers of particular products.
```

Regulations governing ticket applications.

better than turned up for the World Cup.

The arrangements for London were, of necessity, rather more complex so I left them to another friend. He was happy to tag along for a cheap holiday even though he was not interested very much in football and had no tickets. The criteria were economy and convenience. He booked into the corporation hostel in Kentish Town; a sort of cross between a workhouse, prison and youth hostel. The other residents were all either young people on the first rung of the employment ladder and with no money for anywhere better, or else 'old lags' with nowhere else to go. It was downmarket but very cheap – under four pounds for a whole week B&B. After the week we even qualified to stay on longer on a daily basis.

Travel down to London by coach and accommodation at such a basic level meant we could do it all on the cheap – as had to be the case given our very limited resources. I remember how expensive everything generally seemed to be in London, especially the Watneys Red Barrel beer. I'd have loved to have bought more souvenirs but again it was a matter of cost. I never got the one I most wanted, a replica World Cup.

Norman Shiel

Fan 2

I saw all the games in Manchester and Liverpool and then moved to London. I fancied a hotel on the north side of London so I would see a test match as well. There was one single room left in a hotel chosen by chance just three weeks before the competition began. I ended up in the same hotel as the England team. There was no special security then. The England players would be in the lounge watching highlights of other games on the TV.

Tony Sheldon

Varia

I was at that time working for the BBC as an out-of-hours duty manager and my office was adjacent to the accommodation which was occupied by the international media, the BBC being the source for the worldwide distribution of TV pictures. I believe the newly built 'Spur' at television centre was occupied in advance for this purpose before eventually becoming the home of BBC news from Alexandra Palace. Apart from the place buzzing with extra foreigners, I recall only how foul mouthed one particular famous commentator, who shall be nameless, could be when things went wrong or when he didn't get what he wanted.

I was also a special constable based at Hammersmith, which meant I was on duty for the game which was played at the White City. Because of my duties I did not have an uninterrupted opportunity to follow the game, but I do remember it being far from exciting.

I was at the final itself only through the kindness of a former colleague who had a season ticket for the North Eastern group's games but who for some reason could not use his ticket for the final. Obviously I enjoyed the game. I was standing in the enclosure next to the players' tunnel, numbered 111 now. My only real memory of afterwards is, for one of the few times in my life, getting really drunk in a pub near Marble Arch.

Ian Todd

CHAPTER 2

Games before the Final

Germany made light work of beating Switzerland.

I was in my early twenties at the time and living in Leicester. In order to get to any of the games after work it meant being able to drive so a friend and I both decided that we just had to pass our tests and buy cars – which we duly did. We went as a group with other friends to all the group matches at Hillsborough and Villa Park and then on beyond that right through to the final. It meant taking time off work eventually to get to the games that were further away.

I remember the Swiss had lots of fans with cowbells. My memory of Mr Ratin was that he was a magnet for the ball and never had to run. He was the player of the tournament for me. In the Uruguay v. Germany game two were sent off. Helmut Haller should have been in the Royal Ballet. The Germans antagonised their opponents.

At the final I met a little Peruvian chap who was only five feet tall and had my photo taken with him. I still have all my souvenirs and cuttings.

Lionel Blower

Swiss goalkeeper Elsever lends a helping hand.

In 1966 I was a PE teacher at a secondary school in Derbyshire. With a teacher from a neighbouring school we arranged to take the boys to World Cup games. We purchased twelve ten-match tickets, which ensured places at the final, and hired a minibus. It was organised in such a way that everyone saw one game from the group B matches at Aston Villa or Sheffield Wednesday and one game which was a quarter-final or better. I saw Argentina *v*. Spain at Aston Villa and the final at Wembley. I was also fortunate enough to see North Korea *v*. Portugal at Everton as a quarter-final as I went home for the weekend and a friend had a spare ticket. My memories are these:

(Argentina *v*. Spain at Aston Villa, 13 July, k.o. 7.30 p.m.) I remember being impressed by the close control of the Argentine players. Two or three players were able to work their way down the touchline passing the ball even though they were closely marked. The black side of their character was shown when one of their players was sent off, I think, for a scything tackle.

(North Korea *v*. Portugal at Everton on 23 July, k.o. 3.00 p.m.) This was a very exciting game with plenty of goals. Portugal with Eusebio, were firm favourites to win but the North Korea underdogs were strongly supported by the majority of the crowd who were delighted when the North Koreans put two early goals past Periera the Portuguese goalkeeper. Periera had built up

Albrecht of Argentina is sent off and the rest of his team complain to the referee.

a reputation in previous matches in the group as a timewaster by bouncing the ball as he walked around the penalty area. I seem to think FIFA changed the rule about goalkeepers being able to bounce the ball after three steps after the World Cup. The class of the Portugal side told in the second half and they ran out 5-3 winners. I was impressed with Eusebio, who scored four goals and I can still remember his tremendously powerful shot. I don't think I have ever seen anyone hit a ball so hard, even Bobby Charlton.

Roy Beswick

Anything as monumental and historic as the World Cup, in your own land, won by your own team, leaves a body of shared memory interspersed with fragments of your own glimpses back to those glorious days…Nobby Stiles, gap-toothed and grasping his partners together in the defensive wall with minutes to go and England 2-1 up; vainly, because Wolfgang Weber scored to equalize. The agony of those moments before Geoff Hurst's shot off the crossbar was ruled a goal, Uwe Seeler's great sportsmanship in dragging his angry players away from the officials and then Geoff Hurst's final goal and pandemonium.

Those things we all saw and remember but the days and months leading up to the World Cup had their own excitement; the anticipation was almost as good as the reality and still gives me my best memory of World Cup 1966.

The team that nobody knew was North Korea, later to dismiss Italy in ignominy with a goal from Pak Do Ik. They had qualified in a play-off against Australia in Pnom Penh and then retreated north of the 38th parallel to prepare. We all knew and could write about Brazil and Italy and Germany and the rest with scarcely need to check the facts (although, as the old reporter's adage goes, never let the facts stand in the way of a good story) but North Korea was a complete blank.

I was in northern Italy, for the Italy *v.* Argentina game a few weeks before the World Cup when I had a tip (from whom I shall not say, but he attended St Luke's College and later rose to high office within football) that the Koreans were in training in East Germany. So, I flew to Berlin, crossed into East Berlin at checkpoint Charlie, rented a car, received a twenty-four hour visa for East Germany and set off for Gustrow and the Werner Seelenbinder

Russia v. South Korea at Ayrsome Park. The locals took to the mysterious Koreans.

The Russians got off to a comfortable start, beating Korea 3-0.

Bulgarella of Italy is carried off in the disastrous game in which Korea, by winning 1-0, provided the shock result of the tournament.

Left: *Yashin spreads himself*. Right: *The Koreans look totally committed in this tussle for the ball.*

Sportsschule, on the Baltic, not far from the World War Two rocket sites at Peenemunde.

With more luck than judgement, I got there and asked for Herr Direktor. He came out to meet me, a very large, fit-looking man of middle age, grim and forbidding. Did he, I asked, have the North Koreans encamped here? Lengthy silence, then he asked: Did I know Bert Trautmann? Of course, I said, who did not know the brilliant goalkeeper of Manchester City, who played in the Cup Final with a broken neck and who had been a German paratrooper prisoner-of-war before staying on? Well, he said, I was taken prisoner at the same time as Bert Trautmann. He stayed on after the war, I chose to come home – who do you think made the right choice? His rueful look made it clear the question was rhetorical.

In any event, before I could think of a reply, he went on to say yes, the Koreans were here, did I want to meet them, they would be training soon, the third session of a day which had begun with readings from Chairman Mao's Red Book at dawn and so on and so on.

All the Korean players were in the Army. Their officials were officers, their head of delegation a general and all about my age, so I could not help thinking 'I wonder how far away you were, mate, when I was in the Army along the Imjin fifteen years ago?'

But, considering where I was and that there were a lot more of them than there was of me, I kept to the story and what a wonderful and exclusive story it was on the hermits of Asia. I drove like mad back into West Berlin to file the tale and be sure I did not overstay my visa. Like Herr Direktor and Bert Trautmann, I knew which side I preferred to be on.

Looking back over what I have written, I should have said that was my best professional memory.

Clive Toye

An amazing memory of mine from the 1966 World Cup came during the North Korea *v.* Italy match on July 19th at Ayresome Park, Middlesbrough which was won 1-0 by the Koreans. When Pak Do Ik scored the goal a wag in the crowd said 'that's another fucker here' – perhaps a reference to the fact that the Koreans had only managed one goal prior to that in their 1-1 draw against Chile.

F. Furness

My most lasting memory from the 1966 World Cup concerns buying tickets for the three matches at Ayresome Park as my father's Christmas present. He simply could not get over having to pay as much as £1 just to watch a football match. (I wonder what he would have thought now?)

North Korea played all their matches here, so we sort of adopted them as our home team. In the first game they were hammered by Russia. In the next they had learnt things and managed to draw with Chile. When they beat Italy the ground erupted and there was so much cheering and stamping that damage was done to rooms under the stand. We all know how close they came to overcoming Portugal, except for Eusebio.

Miss E. Rowlands

I was only twelve in 1966 but I went to all the games in the North East group and most especially remember being befriended at Ayresome Park by an Italian at the game against Korea. He gave me an Italian flag to wave which meant we were out of it as far as all the other Middlesbrough folk were concerned as they were all squarely behind the Koreans – who won.

I. Short

Pak Do Ik scores the goal that put Italy out of the competition.

As a thirteen-year-old my dad took me to the game between Russia and North Korea at Ayresome Park. I recall watching the game from the new seated area in the East Stand. Russia won 3-0. I still have the two tickets from the game, which was held on Tuesday 12th July, the cost being £1 each. Furthermore, I have held onto a World Cup '66 *Evening Gazette Special Supplement*, price 6d. It contains team details, together with pictures of all the grounds used in the competition and a colour picture of the England squad and also one of Pele.

B. Neale

mates from work. We parked in Denmark Street and walked from there to the ground. There simply wasn't the traffic then and things like that were much easier.

We were hoping to see Yashin play, but he never appeared at Middlesbrough. Russia wiped the floor with little Korea but everyone liked the Koreans and they got their shock result with their one-goal victory over Italy. In those days crowds could mix freely and even change from one end to the other.

J. Dixon

We were living at South Bank at the time of the 1966 World Cup and I was a fairly regular supporter of Middlesbrough and I went to two World Cup games with

In Sunderland at the time of the 1966 World Cup I don't recall there being any Italian restaurants, but there was a café run by an Italian called Tommasitis and a lovely ice cream parlour,

Left: *The Koreans pile on the pressure against Italy at Ayresome Park.* Right: *Pak Seung Zin being escorted from the field by a sailor after the draw with Chile.*

Goalmouth action from the quarter-final between Russia and Hungary at Roker Park.

Notrianni's, which had been there for a number of years. It is now a Macdonalds.

There was also an Italian barbers shop in Low Row near the Empire Theatre. I called in one day during the World Cup and was surprised to find three of the Italian team waiting for their haircuts. Apparently the barber had extended an invitation to the whole team offering free haircuts, and one had obviously accepted. I did not think to ask them for their autographs. They did not speak English but chatted away in Italian to the barber for half an hour. It was a nice memory.

I also remember that some of the CCCP players used to go out in the afternoons and give away little metal badges to pin on coats. The one I was given was a red locomotive with the Russian works name on in yellow. I think this was just a friendly gesture. I kept it for many years but unfortunately lost it in the end.

F. Skinner

I lived approximately $1\frac{1}{2}$ miles from Teeside Airport and the North Koreans were staying at the Tees-side Airport Hotel prior to their three games at Ayresome Park, Middlesbrough, against Italy, Russia and Chile. The twenty-odd thousand crowd really got behind the Koreans against Italy and they won 1-0.

My friends and I used to attend the training ground at the Tees-side Airport after school just to watch the Koreans training. I think that we were all amused that the Koreans were all so small.

B. Day

Completed pages from the tournament programme.

I was fifteen years old in 1966 and on junior forms with my local club Stockport County. A family friend had some good connections and got us tickets for various games. I never knew which ones I'd be going to until just about the last minute.

I saw Bulgaria *v.* Hungary at Old Trafford and then several games at Goodison. I remember the Brazil and Portugal fans at Goodison, all able to speak the same language and all so very passionate. The drums and the noise were amazing but it was all very good-natured. The only violence was on the pitch where the Brazilians, and especially Pele, got kicked to bits.

Brazil were staying at Lymm in Cheshire and while they were in the competition the village became Brazilian with flags everywhere. When they were knocked out the Germans used it as a base for a while before their game in the semi-final against Russia.

I also remember the marvellous quarter-final at Goodison where the little Koreans took a three-goal lead against Portugal. Some Korean fans next to us had a big Korean flag and every time they scored they asked for permission to wave their flag. Before the game the Portuguese players were chatting to fans outside the ground and signing autographs, all very relaxed and informal.

P. Wilkinson

I was convinced we would win long before the tournament started. I just knew Ramsay would take us the final and win.

I had two babies and a 100% mortgage and no money, being on the lowest rung with ICI. I bought the cheapest grade of ten-match ticket in order to make sure of

42

getting a ticket for the final itself. My group games were those at Manchester and Everton.

I saw Pele at Goodison when he was carried off on a rainy evening. My memory of the group games was of there being lots of space at most of them. You could just wander about on the terraces. Pele's games seemed pretty full. In those games the atmosphere seemed quite good, but generally the teams playing had virtually none of their own nationals there as supporters.

D. Jones

I was a spectator at the three group games at Goodison Park. Unfortunately, prior holiday commitments prevented me attending the quarter and semi-finals.

My abiding memory is of the Brazil *v.* Hungary game, which was high on drama and was played in a superb atmosphere. With the enthusiastic crowd urging them on Hungary went on to claim a famous victory in which the highlight was undoubtedly the performance of the centre forward Albert. In a display worthy of any old fashioned number nine, Albert appeared to terrify the ageing Brazilian rearguard. Such was his display that after the game several hundreds of the Goodison crowd congregated outside the main entrance chanting his name. My memory also recalls the bravery of one of the Hungarian defenders who played on despite a damaged shoulder (possibly a broken collar bone), and in an earlier game the brutality of the Portuguese players who

Brazil opened comfortably with a 2-0 defeat of Bulgaria at Goodison.

were determined to, and were allowed to 'knobble' Pele.

R. Condliffe

I would have been about twelve years old then and a fanatical Liverpool supporter – what great times I was going to see! Times were hard in Liverpool in 1966 so having a brother-in-law who worked on the gates at Goodison meant that this scally 'bunked' in to see these great teams and also the colourful supporters.

(Brazil 2 Bulgaria 0) I was in the old Park End behind the goal with all the Brazil fans. I can still see the smiling faces, green tops, waving flags and singing. Oh yes, this was for me. Apart from seeing the great Pele and Garrincha, the fans were the best. At one end, Gwladys Street, all Evertonians; at the Park End, Liverpool and Brazil. The shout went up during a break in the play, 'Everton, Everton' then from the Park End, 'Liverpool, Liverpool'. I can still see the face of this Brazil fan saying, 'Who is this Everton, Liverpool? We shout for Brazil, yes?' Soon it seemed that 50,000 people were shouting 'Brazil, Brazil'. That night was unforgettable; a great night.

(Hungary 3 Brazil 1) I was on cloud nine after the first game so this new Brazil fan could not wait to slide under the turnstile on a cold wet night at Goodison. Pele was the only one people were talking about but in this game a tall lanky man called Albert and a small one called Bene were the names to talk about. I remember looking at the football that was played – fast, skilful and with great goals. You have to remember that at this time all I was used to was a big boot up front; no real skill, although Liverpool

Jose Augusto heads his second goal for Portugal against Hungary. Eusebio is the player with the bandaged head.

Tostoa jumps for joy during the match between Brazil and Hungary.

did go on to get better! After this game I walked home a distance of ten miles as I had no bus fare. I thought 'I'll never see thirteen at this rate!'

(Portugal 3 Brazil 1) I remember being in school when the other kids were saying 'I wish I could go to a match' and I would say, 'Ha! I've been to both games so far and I'm going to the next one 'cos I can get in easy!' Guess what happened? My stupid brother-in-law got the sack Oh no! – Policemen and security men on every gate, 58,000 inside and I'm walking around outside. I'd seen my last match. Unfortunately it was Brazil's last match also; Eusebio saw to that. I did in fact manage to get in for the last twenty minutes and am sorry I did. The once happy Brazilians looked so sad, crying, trying to sell their tickets for the semi-final and final games which they had confidently bought in advance. I walked home sad that day with a tear in my eye.

Never mind, England were still going well. I hoped that Roger Hunt and 'Bally' would keep going well too. I watched most of the other games on next door's black and white television.

I can remember filling in my progress chart; school and lessons just went out the window. It was World Cup only. North Korea beat Italy 1-0, now that was a shock. I was pleased the underdogs won and better still were going to be playing Portugal at Goodison. Should I try to go? Should I try to give my support to the little lads against the giants? No, I stayed at a friend's house with a group.

All we ever did as kids was kick a ball – in the park, in the street, against the wall – bang, bang, bang all day long. This day was no different. My mate's dad must have been in a good mood. He called us all in and said the match was on the television: 'Come on Korea!'

You have to remember those were great days. Six or seven scally kids, short pants, snotty noses but polite kids, good kids, never answered back, swore, robbed nor hurt anyone. So it was crisps, lemonade, nuts and the big match. It seemed it had

The Brazilians celebrate Pele's goal against Hungary.

only just started then 1-0 to Korea! Yes, the shouting goes up in the living room…Korea (clap-clap)…Korea (clap clap). The chairs go flying as it becomes 2-0 then 3-0 to Korea. This is all too much. Never mind Brazil, why could I not have been there for this one? I remember the whole crowd cheering for Korea and everyone was enjoying this but we all know how it ended – 4-3 to Portugal. It was good while it lasted, then back to the wall and bang, bang, bang, bang.

G. Carse

I was a steward at the Bullen Road Stand in 1966 and so I got to see all the games played at Goodison Park. Two things stand out in my memory.

Hungary were playing and it was a dreadful day, raining and the pitch was very wet and slippery. Albert the centre forward played the finest game I had ever seen a centre forward play up to that time. He was so good that the crowd kept chanting his name after the teams had left the pitch at full time. About five minutes later he appeared by himself and did a solo lap of honour to a standing ovation. The Hungarian supporters caused a few smiles. They were all dressed in identical clothes: a trilby, a dark suit, a fawn mackintosh and all carrying brown paper shopping bags from Burton the tailors!

(Portugal *v.* Korea) The Koreans played it like a game of chess in the first half and were leading 3-0 at half time. The Portuguese supporters were crying in the grandstand. In the second half it was a different matter and Portugal ran out comfortable winners by the end.

J. Griffiths

I have been a lifelong Liverpool supporter and I went to all the games at Goodison. I saw Pele's sad treatment and injury and I remember everyone really getting behind the little Koreans in their quarter-final game at Goodison, but Eusebio was just too good for them.

T. Higham

When asked by nephews and younger friends I have always related what turned out to be my biggest disappointment in sport.

From the day I received my tickets right up until kick-off nothing else was spoken off except that Pele was coming to Goodison Park. I stood on the large terrace in front of the main stand (now long gone) and on our left some twenty yards away were several hundred Portuguese fans with flags, banners and so on. The stands right round the ground echoed to the Samba music and the drum beats of the Brazilian fans. The atmosphere was electric with two great teams, and Pele, about to grace our turf.

The reception given to both sides was terrific. They lined up, the referee blew for kick-off and then the Portuguese proceeded to kick the great man off the park. Not only were several crippling fouls committed, but off the ball Pele was subjected to pushes, punches and, I am sure, verbal abuse.

We kept waiting for our football treat to

Antonio Simoes (on the ground) heads his side into the lead against Brazil.

be served up but the 'waiter' was laid low time and time again until finally he was kicked once too often and had to be carried off. Unfortunately the Portuguese fans by me decided this was the occasion for celebrations – a mistake! Around them were numbed and very disappointed scousers (both red and blue), many of whom had paid big money to ensure their ticket to see the great man. I am sorry to say that many a Portuguese fan joined Pele that night in needing medical attention!

In later games Eusebio restored our image of Portuguese football and Lev Yashin gave a goalkeeping display to remember, but I still felt robbed of the opportunity to say that Pele was the greatest I ever saw, as he never really got the chance!

T. Heakin

My younger brother Thomas, who now lives in Australia, and I purchased a book of tickets to four matches prior to the semi-final at Goodison Park. We decided to pick two matches each with me having Portugal *v.* Korea and Hungary *v.* Brazil and Thomas having Portugal *v.* Brazil and one other.

My memories of the Portugal match involve hundreds if not thousands of North Koreans in the upper Bullen stand and their team going three nil up in the first twenty-five minutes I think. I was eighteen at the time and it was my first experience of World Cup football close up. The smiles and happiness of the Korean supporters was a great sight to see, until the great Eusebio took over and scored four goals, one a penalty I think, and one particular goal scored at the Gwladys Street goal. I have yet to see a footballer between then and now hit a ball as hard. I have seen the matches on the television over the years about 1966 and I think David Coleman was commentating on that game for the BBC. For that goal he said he had never seen anything like it in his life. Eusebio scored four goals, with Portugal winning 5-3 in the end.

My second game was Hungary *v.* Brazil and, because of my age, the Brazilian supporters and Hungarian supporters outside the ground before the match provided my first experience of colour and drums, with the dress of the people really something to behold. Seeing these people from other parts of the world, happy and enjoying themselves, made me think what football meant to them and why they travelled so far for just ninety minutes.

The actual match was won 3-1 by Hungary and they had a centre forward called Florian Albert; what a great player he was. The thing that struck me about Eusebio and Florian Albert was the speed they had along with their ball control awareness. The football pitch was treated like a snooker table with size being the governing factor.

A. McDonald

I was twelve years of age in 1966 and went to the game between North Korea and Portugal. Korea went 3-0 up within about half an hour. I ended up sitting in a little cage during the game with the unused players! At the end of the game Eusebio picked me up and put me on the shoulders of Torres for a photograph. He was a giant of a man. It was quite something for a twelve year old to be held onto by such as

English referee Jim Finney dismisses Troche of Uruguay

Eusebio and Torres. It was the only game I went to. Roy McFarland's cousin got us the tickets.

D. Hughes

I went from Holyhead with a friend to four games at Goodison. I still have the ticket application form with the price, £2 12s 6d for the four games.

The Brazil *v.* Hungary match was the most skilful game I have ever seen live. I felt privileged to see it; it was a great night – Pele was playing. We were amongst the Hungarian fans who were in tears by the end. It was pouring with rain pretty well all the time. After the game we waited for the players to come out and I remember touching them as they went by. The Brazil players looked so sullen.

At the time we were coming back home the *Sound of Music* was on the radio. We'd seen the *Sound of Music* on the field. I just had to stop and phone somebody to say how good it had been.

Brazil versus Bulgaria was also good. I was right behind Garrincha when he bent a free kick like nothing I had ever seen before. I also saw North Korea *v.* Portugal and that was a funny sort of a game, but magical. You tended to feel it was all just unreal when the Koreans built up their three-goal lead but with Eusebio the main course was still to come.

That was the best two weeks of my life; The streets were all decked out.

G. Davies

I watched Liverpool from the late fifties and my brother was an Everton fan. I remember that we all watched the opening game in 1966 on the television and thought that if that was what was to come it would be all defence and few goals.

Next day we flew down to Jersey for our

holidays and saw a few matches on the television in the hotel lounge. There were some great games such as that between Hungary and Brazil when Farkas scored that volley with one arm in a sling. All hell broke loose but there was no 'my club is better than yours'. Everybody watched the matches in a fantastic atmosphere.

When we arrived back in Liverpool we heard that there might be tickets left for the semi-final between Russia and Germany. We went up to Everton's ground and got two, much to our surprise. The match was awful. Both teams made it a battleground and hacked each other to pieces. Somebody got sent off, I forget who. The one consolation was that we saw the great Lev Yashin in goal for Russia – I think it was his last game.

A. Bell

I saw Korea *v*. Portugal with the big lad Torres and, of course, Eusebio. A group of us went up from Shropshire and it was a good day out. Korea had paralysed Portugal in the early part of the game, then Eusebio turned on the heat and Portugal fought their way back into it. For the final I stopped off on my way south for a holiday and watched the game on the television at my brother's house in Bristol. I always preferred standing at matches.

T. Myatt

Around that time I was in my mid-twenties and playing amateur football in the fourth team of a club, MEC (Manchester Education Committee), whose first team played in the Lancashire Amateur League and who were affiliated through the Lancashire Football Association to the FA. As a result, at the beginning of the 1965/66 season all players with the club were offered the chance to buy a set of tickets. I chose the most expensive option, entitling me to watch all the games played in the North West (at Goodison Park and Old Trafford), and the final. I can't remember how much I paid, but what a marvellous investment it turned out to be.

The North West group was made up of Bulgaria, Brazil, Hungary and Portugal. For some reason I didn't get to any of the Bulgaria games. The first match I saw was Hungary *v*. Portugal at Old Trafford, and the way Portugal played was a revelation to me – fast, seemingly telepathic passing movements, great individual skills and explosive finishing. Eusebio was outstanding. One incident, although not obviously special, has always stayed clear in my memory. Portugal got a corner on the right, near where I was standing. Eusebio, wearing a white bandage round his head following a clash earlier in the game, came over to take the kick. I saw him make a sign to Torres, the very tall striker, and I saw Torres nod in acknowledgement. I thought 'He knows just what he wants to do, he knows he's got the accuracy to do it, and Portugal are going to score'. Sure enough, Eusebio's corner kick evaded the goalkeeper and Torres climbed high at the far post to head a simple goal.

Portugal and Eusebio were just as good in their game against Brazil at Goodison. Pele started the game but was obviously not match fit, the Portuguese defenders were not at all gentle with him, and Brazil and Pele really made little impression on me.

The Hungary *v*. Brazil game at Goodison was exciting, although the quality of the football was not as good as in the Portugal games. The goal by Farkas for Hungary stands out in my memory – he had had a wretched game against Portugal and I don't recall him doing much else in the Brazil game, but he got a chance where it looked extremely easy to slice the ball badly or hit it well wide, and I felt sure one of these two was going to happen. Instead he hit the ball perfectly and scored a superb goal.

After the group matches were over, the next game was Portugal *v.* North Korea at Goodison. At the same time, England were playing Argentina, and throughout our exciting game we were kept up to date over the PA system with events at Wembley – it sounded pretty poor – still 0-0 for most of the time, then an announcement that the Argentina captain had been sent off, and at long last a goal for England. Meanwhile…

North Korea were playing like no professional team I had ever seen. It seemed almost like watching very young schoolboys playing – wherever the ball went the whole team seemed to follow. However their players could hold the ball well, and Portugal seemed completely bewildered by their bizarre tactics. Even when North Korea went 3-0 up though, it seemed only a matter of time before Portugal would take control and wipe out their lead. And of course that was how it turned out; the Koreans had no answer to Eusebio and panicked every time he ran at them, and it ended 5-3 to Portugal. Another marvellous match.

The next and last match in the North West was memorable only for its dreadfulness. It was West Germany's semi-final – I can't remember now whether their opponents were Czechoslovakia or USSR – which they won 2-1. I was so bored with the game that I left while the score was still

Pele's tournament is over; the greatest player in the world had been fouled throughout the competition.

2-0 and missed the last goal. There was no flow to the match, just stoppage after stoppage, and it compared very poorly with everything I had seen so far.

Watching the England-Portugal game on television was an experience of mixed emotions. Of course I wanted England to win, and was happy that they did, but at the same time I was sorry to see Portugal go out. If England had been knocked out of the competition earlier, I would have supported Portugal all the way to the final.

D. Roberts

I was eighteen years old in 1966, in my A level year. My mother and my aunt, who brought me up, got for me as a present for *taking* my A levels – regardless of the results – a ten-match ticket for all the games in London. I still have all the tickets and they are very special.

I can recall the excitement of the first day; going from Euston to Wembley Central then feeling the atmosphere building up during the walk to the stadium. I was generally interested in football and had been a Manchester United fan since their 1957 Cup Final. After the build up of excitement for the occasion of the opening, the first game itself was something of a disappointment. There wasn't so much of an atmosphere at that game itself but that was very much something which grew steadily as the tournament went on.

Probably the thing that really brought it all to life was Charlton's wonderful goal in England's second game against Mexico. From that moment on the mood became positive and the whole country came onboard and began to believe in Alf's prophecy. I recall the White City game being played in atrocious weather conditions but still attracting a good crowd.

For the quarter-final there was good weather. I recall Ratin towering over the little referee. Hurst headed his goal at the far end – I was always at the tunnel end and began to wonder when we would see some goals at our end! By then I was beginning to get to know the people around me in the same pen. From where I was it was clear from Alf's reaction just how angry he was.

By the semi-final I was locked into a 'lucky routine' for my journey to the games and could not bring myself to risk changing it. Portugal had rather taken over from Brazil as the class side with stars like Eusebio, Torres and Simoes. My personal favourite from that side was Simoes, as he was a left winger like myself. I always

Connelly leads an England attack during the game against Uruguay.

Jack Charlton puts in a header against Uruguay. Roger Hunt is the other England player.

The Uruguay defence prepares for action during their game with England.

Enrique Borja scores to give Mexico the lead against France at Wembley.

believed we would win the semi final. Afterwards I went home exultant and by this stage even my mum and auntie, who were not really football fans, were getting caught up in the excitement of the World Cup.

D. Davies

In 1966 I had just left school and was working at Croydon's planning department. I and two friends decided to get a season ticket for the event but we had left it a bit late and we could only get tickets for England's qualifying group games plus the Wembley quarter-final. We travelled up to Marylebone by car/tube then took the British Rail train up to Wembley Stadium station. This was a station built for the original Wembley Exhibition and is no longer there now. Typically of this country, everything had been left until the last minute and the tarmac was still sticking to one's feet as we arrived for the first match, against Uruguay.

We got there quite early in order to soak up the atmosphere and see the merchandising stalls, which were a tacky collection. This was before mass merchandising as we know it now. There were scarves and rosettes but no replica shirts. Still, I got myself a World Cup Willie car sticker. The opening ceremony was a bit of an anti-climax with lots of school kids walking round holding national flags as I remember. The game was quite good with England piling on lots of pressure but the Uruguayan defence was exceptionally well organised and skilful, playing the ball out of

Jubilation after Enrique Borja's (number 20) goal against France at Wembley.

The White City Stadium, where the Uruguay v. France game was played because Wembley was not available. The venue was also the operational headquarters for the 1966 World Cup finals.

the penalty area and keeping possession but rarely getting it into England's half. It was all rather frustrating.

We also saw the other group games but I can't remember all that much apart from Bobby Charlton's spectacular shot against Mexico. The only other game I remember was for the venue as much as anything else. That was the game at the White City, Uruguay v. France. Apparently the FA wanted to play that at Wembley too but Wembley Stadium Limited wouldn't allow them to as it would have clashed with their greyhound night! Imagine it, dogs taking preference over the World Cup – I ask you!

I'd never been to the White City. Queens Park Rangers had played there for a little while but apparently the atmosphere was awful. Remember they were a Third Division team at the time. It wasn't much better with 40,000 spectators, mostly French, watching this game either as there was both an athletics track and a dog track between the spectators and the pitch. The game seemed miles away. I can't even remember the score. The quarter-final against Argentina was quite a game, especially with Ratin being sent off and refusing to leave: another well organised South American defence until Hurst's brilliant header.

We thought we'd seen all the games we were likely to see when I received a letter from Wembley saying that some tickets were available for the semi-final and the third/fourth place play-off game, and our previous purchase gave us priority for obtaining these. We thus went to the game against Portugal along with the King of Jordan, not that we sat together! Eusebio played for them that night but England were

Julio Cortes of Uruguay about to fire the ball past French goalkeeper Marcel Aubour and put his side into a 2-0 lead.

A delighted Cortes turns to recieve the embraces of his delighted team-mates.

Bobby Charlton (number 9) turns away as his shot finds the net in the game against Mexico.

Mexican goalkeeper Calderon (number 12) has just been beaten by a Roger Hunt (21) strike.

just unstoppable. In fact, Portugal were fortunate to get there as I remember during the England *v*. Argentina game the score from their game against North Korea going up on the scoreboard, and a massive cheer going up at Wembley every time the Koreans scored.

The third/fourth place game was a non-event, no atmosphere and no interest from the Wembley crowd with a dour Soviet Union team playing against Portugal. I think Lev Yashin was in goal but I could be mistaken. I can't even remember the result.

S. Saul

In 1966 I was quite a young man, only having left school for a few years, and was working as a trainee surveyor. Leading up to the World Cup, I realised that not only was the national team playing well but the football at club level was superb. It was, of course, the clubs that were feeding the national team with players. I went home and said to my father that the way English football was at that point of time, there was a very good chance that England would win the World Cup. I remember vividly that he laughed at me and said that I didn't know what I was talking about. I was so convinced I contacted a few of my friends that I played football with and a group of about six of us decided to endeavour to obtain tickets. This we did.

I duly went to my employers and booked the dates, pointing out that I had a complete set of tickets for the Wembley venue. My employers granted me the two weeks holiday but refused to give me the Friday off as an extra day. I was only entitled to two weeks holiday. This meant that I would miss the first game – which turned out to be the infamous game between England and Argentina involving a gentleman known as Ratin. I wasn't confident enough in those days to argue with my employers and push them to give me the extra two days I needed and had to settle for missing it.

In those days, I was always the last to book and take my holiday. All the rest of the staff came first. I ended up taking two week's leave in late September, or early October, when the weather was poor and there was nobody about. I was, therefore, absolutely astounded when about three weeks before the World Cup one of the partners in the firm came to me and asked me if I would move my holiday. I exploded like Mount Vesuvius. I told him he could sack me if he wished but I had tickets for the World Cup – which by then were like gold dust – and I'd rather he would sack me than miss the games. I had suddenly found my self-confidence. Needless to say, he backed off and my holiday dates were protected.

The atmosphere at the games was magnificent. Every team had its supporters and they could be seen not only at the games but in the rest of London at various times of day or night. National dress was much in evidence and particularly noticeable were the Mexicans. There was a tremendous atmosphere and, of course, in those days spectators of opposing teams could still mix together, united in a love of football – a far cry from the tribal conflicts that were to erupt with later generations of so-called football supporters. Much of what happened during the World Cup is well documented but there are certain aspects which are probably not known.

Firstly, most of the English supporters were confident that the England team would go far in the competition. This belief was not founded on blind patriotism but in the knowledge that English football was probably the best in the world at that point

Bobby Moore heads for the Mexican goal. This effort went just inches wide of the mark.

Charlton leaves the field lost in thought.

of time. After all, one of the greatest goalscorers of the era, Jimmy Greaves, could not even make the England side. There was also a new manager called Alf Ramsey, whose ways were somewhat mysterious but seemed to be successful. Those of us who support Torquay United remembered him well. Only once in their lifetime did Torquay United ever look like getting into the old Second Division, they had a superb side. They failed to obtain this goal on goal average alone, being beaten by a club, later to become famous, known as Ipswich. The manager at that time was a certain Alf Ramsey. Torquay went into oblivion whereas Alf Ramsey and Ipswich went on to much greater things. This is the difference between success and failure.

Another thing that may not be documented is that, almost universally, the spectators in Wembley felt that there was only one team to be beat. This was not Germany but Portugal. We all felt that whoever could beat Portugal would win the competition. Many of us in the crowd felt that the real final was not against Germany but was the previous match. There was one moment in the game when Eusebio broke through and only had the goalkeeper to beat but failed to do so due to a very weak shot (unusual for him), which the falling 'keeper was able to put a hand to. When that opportunity was lost to Portugal, everybody in the crowd said we'll now win the World Cup. There are two other moments that are worth recording.

The first was that most of the sympathy at Wembley went to the Mexico team, they were seen as rank outsiders and were perceived to be a struggling force at that level. Their supporters were superb, always smiling and very friendly. Their games did

Mexican goalkeeper Antonio Carvajal covers his face as his side miss yet another chance against Uruguay in the match at Wembley.

not attract big crowds, consequently individual shouts could be clearly heard in the stadium. There was one game, and I cannot recall who the opponents were, where Mexico were clearly struggling and I personally started cheering every pass that Mexico made that went correctly – three passes resulted in three cheers. If the ball was finally intercepted by the opponents, I booed. Before I knew it, that form of cheering and chanting was taken up by my colleagues and the people in the crowd around me. It then spread all the way around Wembley stadium. The practice then spread throughout English football in the years to follow. Nobody believes me, but I always claim to have originated that idea back in Wembley on that day. In the English League in later years such chanting became more vindictive. One final remembrance with respect to Mexico relates to the goalkeeper. When they finally went out of the competition he was, I believe, the oldest player in the tournament, and about to retire. He was seen to kiss both uprights and then fall on his knees and kiss the pitch. That was his farewell to football.

The second occurrence which is worth recording happened in another game. I cannot remember the game that was unfolding at Wembley. Indeed, I cannot even remember if it was an England game. What I do recall was that at the time another match was being played and that was Portugal versus North Korea. North Korea were very much the minnows of the competition and they exceeded everybody's expectations by getting as far as they did. At Wembley, right up in the gods, was a sign which was informing the crowd of the score of other games. There were little men in white coats – they were little because of the distance – who would walk along a gantry and take down a zero and put up a one when somebody scored. The whole of Wembley was watching this gantry because we expected Portugal to make mincemeat of North Korea. The game had not been going very long when we noticed the little man in the white coat beginning to walk along the gantry. I turned to my colleagues and said 'Here we go, Portugal have scored already'. To my amazement and to the amazement of the whole of Wembley, he walked past Portugal and took down the zero against North Korea and put up a one. Immediately a buzz went around Wembley and we half lost interest in the game that was going on in front of us. Everybody started talking about the unexpected nature of that scoreline. The crowd were still talking when off the little man set again, I turned to my colleagues and said, 'I knew it couldn't last'. Beyond belief the little man walked past the Portugal sign again, took down the one and put up a three. North Korea had gone from 1-0 to 3-0 in almost as many minutes. At this the Wembley crowd absolutely erupted. We couldn't believe it. Those with radios in the crowd confirmed that, indeed, the score was 3-0. The Wembley crowd started cheering. Afterwards seeing recordings of the game I was actually watching at Wembley, I vividly recall Kenneth Wolstenholme saying, during his commentary, that he did not know what the crowd were so excited and cheering about. I could have told him that clearly in his commentary box he was isolated from what was going on in the crowd. Of course, it couldn't last, given time Portugal began to score goals and eventually beat North Korea comprehensively. The Wembley crowd were so excited for a while, however, because, as I have said earlier Portugal were seen as the main adversary in preventing England from winning.

K. Metcalfe

Mexico failed to score against Uruguay – this shot shows the South American 'keeper saving in style.

The Uruguay penalty area is crowded as the South Americans demonstrate defence in depth.

Anontio Carvajal is congratulated at the end of his last ever World Cup game.

Carvajal bids farewell as he exits from his fifth World Cup tournament.

I did attend all the matches at Wembley plus one at the White City. I was, at that time, a struggling junior bank official in my early twenties with a young family and could only afford the cheapest entrance tickets. I remember that some months before the finals I applied for five season tickets (for myself and four friends), all of which I duly received. The season tickets were, in fact, individual tickets for each match contained in a little folder. Somewhere hidden away I still have all the tickets in the original wallet.

The five of us met at my house in Burnham before every game. Only one of us was the proud possessor of a car (a company one) so he was forced to undertake all the driving. It is a good job there was no drink driving law in those days because the first two of many pints were consumed once the car was parked just off Wembley High Street.

At the ground we stood high up in the stand behind the goal at the Western end of the stadium and we had a surprisingly good view with plenty of room. During the tournament we became quite good friends with the people who stood in the same area. After the match ended we never failed to retrieve the car, drive a couple of miles and consume several more pints of beer before continuing the journey home.

The tournament was, of course, the greatest football experience of my life. I vividly remember the opening ceremony, the Bobby Charlton goals, and those later

Hunt scores against France.

on scored by Hurst. Also there was Ratin's sending off and, most of all, the final itself.

J. Collier

I travelled up from Bristol for the early game between England and Uruguay. I thought it was very poor and really couldn't imagine that England would do very well at all in the rest of the competition based on what I saw that day.

Alan Hobbs

I remember going to Wembley with my friend for the semi-final game just to keep him company. He had a ticket and I did not as I was not especially interested in football although I had seen a few of the games in the North East at Roker Park. Not far from Wembley a complete stranger asked how we were placed for tickets and when he found out that I didn't have one he just handed his spare one over without wanting any money at all for it. I thought it rather a waste at the time. For the third/fourth place play-off game I went in similar circumstances and this time ended up buying one of the 7s 6d tickets for ten shillings so I got to see that game too. I didn't bother going to the final.

Otherwise my memories of the World Cup mostly revolve around organising the trip to London for myself and my friend, who was something of a fanatic. We stayed in a council hostel for next to nothing. After the final we met up in central London, went to see the Black and White Minstrel show at the Victoria Palace, had a meal and got back to the hostel sometime after midnight.

The one other thing I can still recall is the quip someone made when my friend was looking for me outside Wembley before one of the games. He asked someone if they had seen a short, stocky character on his way to Wembley and got the reply, 'Do you mean World Cup Willie?'

A. Wilson

I have been a life-long Fulham supporter since my first game in 1935 and I bought a season ticket for all ten games in the London area. In my view, the semi-final against Portugal was the game of the tournament, certainly of the ones I saw. I felt physically shattered after that game as did all those from my family who were with me. I could have sweated buckets in the last ten minutes of the game just waiting for the final whistle yet enjoying the quality of the game. I was standing behind the goal and followed Charlton's rocket second goal all the way into the net. I also have vivid memories of another Charlton piledriver against Mexico, and of the turgid game against Argentina, who were dubbed 'animals' by Ramsay.

K. Dowling

I had a season ticket for all the England group games at Wembley plus the other London games down to and including the final and have fondest memories of that three-week period.

The Argentinian defence make life difficult for England using whatever means they can.

Moore, a model of concentration.

Referee Kreitlein is adamant that Ratin must take his punishment.

Kreitlein rushes to intervene after a clash leaves Jack Charlton sprawling.

A treasured and amusing memory was being at Wembley for the game with Argentina. In those days the half times of the other matches played on the same afternoon, including the ongoing scores, were posted high on a gantry over the terrace at one end of the ground by two men in white coats. The roar that greeted Portugal 0 North Korea 1 was tremendous. Some few minutes later the white-coated attendant set off again to amend the score. A sympathetic buzz went up in expectation of a Portugal equaliser but no! Down came the one and up went a three – Portugal 0, North Korea 3 – the stadium erupted. I'm not sure if the players at Wembley realised the reason for the crowd hysteria. Ultimately of course, order was restored and Portugal recovered to win 5-3. I still treasure that moment on Sat 23rd July.

N. Killick

Kreitlein leaves Ratin in no doubt about his sending off.

After graduating from Southend I had become a Fulham fan. I had tickets for all the London games having got my tickets through an advertisement on the back of the *Daily Express*. I have kept a variety of contemporary souvenirs including my receipt for my tickets at £4 1s and my tournament programme fully annotated. I myself only went to the game England actually played in and sold tickets for the others to my friends.

I went to the games early with a picnic to soak up the atmosphere and wait for the players to arrive. Then I could go into the ground, still nice and early, and, being a short lady, find a good spot from which to see, and enjoy the build up of atmosphere inside the stadium. While having my sandwiches on the grass near the players tunnel where the buses went in I met Bobby and Jackie Charlton's mum doing much the same thing. We met up there three times in all. I remember her saying how nice it was for Jackie to have got to the top as Bobby was much more used to these big occasions. I got on well with her and felt she just wanted to enjoy the build up in the same way as the rest of us. After the games I just went home in a state of elation but remember generally both going to and coming away from games I chatted to lots of fans from all over the place. It was altogether a friendly atmosphere.

Mrs V. Asher

Ratin towers above the referee, but his World Cup is over.

Hurst soars up to head for goal.

As the header sails into the net, England reach the semi-finals for the first time.

West German striker Held (number 10) is pictured scoring his side's first goal against Switzerland at Hillsborough.

At the time of my service at Wembley Police Station, I was PC359Q attached to QD (the code for Wembley Police Station). I was twenty-two years of age at the time and was employed as a Beat Officer and Light Weight Motorcyclist, riding Velocette LE200 water cooled machines.

I had absolutely no interest in football whatsoever. Obviously, working as a policeman in Wembley provided a dearth of opportunity to attend matches on a regular basis. the highlight of the calendar being the FA Cup final with up to 100,000 people attending the match. This was before safety requirements took a number of spaces away.

There were plenty of officers attempting to exchange their night duties for days and I duly obliged and worked nights. This provided me the opportunity to escape the hysteria which seemed to have gripped Wembley and the nation. I worked a 10 p.m. to 6 a.m. shift for three weeks and thereby missed most of the action. My only required interest was during my night shift, when I was employed on the 'Reserve Duty', which was an odd expression which described the person who worked inside and sifted paper and took telephone calls. This necessity of interest required that I collate the crowd and traffic statistics and send them to 'the yard' by teleprinter every night. The enforced use of the teleprinter was very much a baptism by fire.

On my return to day duty, it was all over. Never in my service did I attend a single football match at the 'twin towers'.

Peter J. Dale

I have been a Cardiff City supporter for most of my life. I was living and working in London at the time of the World Cup in 1966. I was fortunate enough to see all of

Ramsay stops Cohen from exchanging shirts after the Argentina game.

DAY EIGHT

ANIMALS!

says Alf as England reach semi-finals

Ramsay's words become headlines and he is forced to apologize.

Haller scores for Germany against Russia in the semi-final at Goodison.

England's group games against Uruguay, Mexico and France and after that I also managed to get to the quarter-final against Argentina. I couldn't get tickets for the semi-final or the final, however.

I remember being down in the West End on the night of the final – what an atmosphere. The traffic was at a standstill and the flags were waving and all the cars were hooting their horns in rotation. I recall that there were lots of people in the fountains in Trafalgar Square. The atmosphere was very good-natured in those days, both at the games and afterwards.

I still have my official programme from the tournament with all the details which I filled in myself.

M. Hughes

Apart from the final itself, the only other match I was able to attend was the game between England and Argentina when they had a player sent off – unheard of in those days. I was seated above the tunnel and most of the crowd stood up and applauded the courage of the referee and booed the player as he went down the tunnel.

C. Poole

I remember that there was an advertisement in the *Daily Express* which gave details about how to go about getting World Cup tickets. I just applied and got a ten-match ticket. I saw all England games. I still have a World Cup tee shirt – which I tell the lads in the pub was my dad's in case it dates me too much! I sometimes get it out and put it on for 'big screen' games. In those days I was living in Swindon and I could

Yashin, the legendary Russian goalkeeper, dives at the feet of Seeler.

leave work there at 5.30 p.m., get a train to Paddington and go to Wembley in time for an evening game. I still have all my tickets.

A. Britton

I was thirty at the time of the World Cup in 1966 and had been a season ticket holder at Chelsea since the early fifties. I bought a ten-match ticket for the London group for about £21 for really good seats. I remember Nobby Stiles made himself unpopular with the French fans during England's game against France. The French fans took against him because of the hardness of his play, as they saw it.

The opening ceremony was much more low key than it would be now. The best

Haller, scorer of some vital goals for Germany.

game of all was the semi-final with Portugal. At the Argentine game I remember being struck by how small the referee was compared to the players. I had the same seat for every game at Wembley; lower tier, left of the goal where Peters scored in the final.

A. Norman

I was fourteen in 1966 and got a block of ten tickets for all the games in London. I think my dad got them through the *Daily Mirror*. I remember coming home on the tube from one game at the White City and being asked by a total stranger if I had a ticket for the England v. Mexico game. I said no because my dad had decided to give my sister the chance to go to that game on 'my' ticket, and so this stranger just gave me his ticket. It was for the next price range up from our usual ones. I ended up right behind Charlton's superbly struck goal.

I. Dix

I was attached to the London Liaison Committee when asked to assume responsibility for public information services. Queries were answered and printed material supplied from a total of seventy-eight staff distributed among the offices of the Reed Paper Group at 82 Piccadilly and kiosks at Gatwick and Heathrow arrival areas, as well as several of London's mainline railway termini. To maintain the supervision and organisation I was allocated one of the pool car fleet provided by the BMC.

Looking back in my file of souvenirs and documents I am struck by the relative crudity of documentation – on moderate quality foolscap paper with text laid down via skin stencils, both of which are now defunct. One exception was the detailed protocol for the opening ceremony, which took the form of a printed booklet. It and its accompanying less formally produced document had some time intervals – particularly when the Queen was involved – in half-minutes.

Some personal highlights of the time for me included eating in the White City restaurant while watching France beat Uruguay in the only game which took place at that now lost venue. I have never asked or explored but I wonder if any commemorative plate exists anywhere on what was the footprint of that great symbol, and I think of its relatively recent wanton destruction as the most monumental symbol of the way politicians of all colours have stood aside and allowed the disposal of green fields now denied to sport and doubtless never to return.

Another was the fracas in an eight-minute stoppage, which followed the despatch of Antonio Ratin by referee Rudolf Kreitlein, and Alf Ramsay's subsequent injudicious comment after the game, 'We still have to produce our best football. It will come against the right type of opposition, a team who come to play football and not act as animals'.

A third was the Brazilian party's disappointment and complaints on arrival at the Crystal Palace National Recreation Centre– a holding site after elimination and *en route* for home after leaving Goodison Park – in the late evening of July 21st. One had to have some sympathy given the spartan nature of the 'cells' (for they were but little more) and for the fact that just about the only food which could be found in the restaurant was packets of crisps, it being declared 'too late for sustenance'. Their *chef de mission* declared a stay beyond overnight was intolerable, and emergency arrangements were made with the only hotel able to take them, then known as the Alexandra National, in Seven Sisters Road, N4.

Finally, I recall dining at the Kensington Palace Hotel where the North Koreans were accommodated after arrival from Goodison Park and their defeat by Portugal after a gallant 3-1 lead at half time (following the astonishing 1-0 defeat of Italy with a goal from Pak Doo Ik, whose name became a watchword in the weeks after). When the team entered the dining room the entire company gave them a standing applause.

W. Goss, AFA

When the World Cup came to England in July 1966 I was just a twelve year old football mad young boy. I don't think I realised what a lucky lad I was, because here I was living a mile away from Wembley Stadium with the Worlds' greatest football championship only days away from its official opening. What I do know is that

Eusebio scores from the penalty spot in the semi-final against England.

One great striker congratulates another; Eusebio and Bobby Charlton after the semi-final at Wembley.

every penny of my paper round wages was going fast on all the magazines and World Cup Willie paraphernalia that the shops were selling!

I can remember making the short walk to Wembley stadium and walking around what amounted to a small World Cup souvenir market, held on ground just beneath the twin towers, just about every evening. To say that I could have spent a fortune is an understatement. The item I was desperate to buy was a replica of the Jules Rimet trophy but at 17/6 this was out of the question, so I had to make do with various World Cup badges (only one still survives in my collection today), rosettes of all the competing nations and various posters (reproduced in a football magazine last year). Unfortunately the rosettes and posters have long since disappeared, how I wish I still had them.

Other items that I still have are the original World Cup Willie scrapbooks that I filled with pictures of all the competing countries player photographs plus a few newspaper reports. What today's memorabilia collectors would give to have the opportunity to go back in time and look through and purchase items form this Aladdin's cave. One evening I can even remember walking along side some of the Uruguayan players who themselves were looking to buy mementos to take home.

How could you top being so near to the heart of the World Cup – well it happened the day before the first match of the tournament, England v. Uruguay. My uncle arrived and gave me a small white envelope with just a few words written in red, 'World Championship – Jules Rimet Cup England – 1966 Season Ticket'. Not quite grasping the enormity of what I had just been handed I quickly opened it to find tickets for every match at Wembley, yes that's all the group matches, quarter-final, semi-final, third place play off and the unbelievable World Cup final. Obviously at that moment in time I couldn't have realised that I was going to be one of the luckiest football fans in Britain and be part of that historic day in English football.

Well today I still have that little white envelope and its contents as my favourite souvenir of 1966, or maybe the memories are!

M. Perrin

Eusebio in tears – so near and yet so far.

Charlton (number 9) turns away after scoring against Portugal in the semi-final.

Germany beat Russia in a dour semi-final at Goodison Park.

I applied in January for a season ticket to stand at all ten London games (nine at Wembley, one at the White City) never imagining that England would win through to the final stages – let alone win the competition. It cost seven guineas and was a lot of money for a young person. There were two prices for standing and this was the dearer one, supposedly giving a better view. I was standing at one end of the pitch – the opposite end to the tunnel from which all the players emerged – underneath the large *Radio Times* sign, which was I think the only advertisement that appeared on TV! The England games attracted huge crowds but I do not recall ever feeling at all frightened or threatened. By contrast the one game at The White City (Uruguay/France) seemed sadly lacking in atmosphere, with a crowd of only 40,000 separated from the pitch by an athletics track.

When attending the games I had to go straight from the office as there wasn't time to get home and back again. Girls did not wear trousers to work in those days so I remember having to disappear into the Ladies to change before going to the football, which attracted much amused comment. I had bought a Hessian bag in a sale for 10s and it proved to be far more useful than any of my smart leather handbags. In it I had sandwiches, a squashable purse and a plastic mac. On arrival at the ground the bag was ideal for sitting on, to eat my packed meal, having staked my claim on my chosen place on the terrace. It was thirteen stops on the tube back to Victoria, then a train ride home so I got back very late but if I hurried I would arrive just in time to see the highlights of the day's games on TV. Like everyone else I remember being delighted by the antics and unexpected success of the North Koreans and enthralled by the goals of the man who I consider to be the greatest ever footballer – Eusebio.

Obviously, however, my main memories are of the England fixtures. The first game against Uruguay was a rather boring stalemate, an anticlimax to the razzamatazz of the opening ceremony and all the papers were full of doom and gloom the next day. I have personal reasons for remembering the next England game, against Mexico, as my best friend held her engagement party that day. Well she was my best friend until I announced that I might not make it as I would be attending a football match and might not be able to get there in time! Some of the Mexican fans came dressed in sombreros, which looked very colourful. The only thing I recall about the next England tie, with France, was the incessant chanting of the French fans, which I spent most of the time trying to decipher and translate. I decided that they were saying 'Allez-vous en, allez-vous en, allez' – but I never did discover if I was right!

There was plenty of time in the long wait before kick-off for supporters to discuss the latest team selections and if we hadn't won the cup most Londoners would have blamed Sir Alf for not risking recalling the injured Jimmy Greaves into the team for the final stages. Then, as now, many of us were prejudiced against players from Northern teams. Roger Hunt took a lot of stick – I nicknamed him 'Elbows' because he seemed to run with them sticking out – how would he have fared in today's game with its harsh interpretation of this? Of course George Cohen was the best full-back ever, especially as far as I was concerned being a fanatical Fulham supporter!

Brazil's reign ends

THE BRILLIANT era in which Brazil coached the world to a new kind of football moved surely towards its end at Goodison Park last night. By losing to Portugal they almost certainly surrendered the World Cup they have held for the past eight years.

Fancied as favourites by many, the Brazilians crashed out in the first phase – leaving many fans stranded

J. L. Manning writes

in PAGE 16: "Arrangements for the World Cup quarter-finals should be changed immediately if England qualify this evening. They are ridiculous as they stand"

Arrangements generally went off pretty smoothly, but some very public doubts were expressed.

The quarter final game against Argentina was my first real experience of witnessing abusive and violent behaviour on a football field – of course we didn't have such things at Fulham! Ratin was the culprit and Alf Ramsey's famous branding of the team as 'animals' hit the media headlines.

The semi-final against Portugal I still consider to have been the finest game of football I have ever seen. It was a magnificent game and I still feel privileged to have been there. I have another personal memory of what happened after this match. My father had obtained a ticket to sit in the stand and we had arranged to meet afterwards to travel home together. Our rendezvous was supposed to be outside the Empire Pool but we hadn't specified which end of it. This was rather silly as it is not easy to find one person amongst a crowd of 90,000. We later found out that our antics must have resembled a Brian Rix farce with Dad pacing up and down one side, with me anxiously looking for him on the other! At one point I ventured inside to ask a commissionaire if he had seen a man of Dad's description. We later worked out that Dad must have then been outside the entrance that I had just left! We never did manage to meet and both finally got home very late to find Mum extremely worried that something must have happened to us.

Mrs P. Chaston

I had a great time, all be it very handicapped. It all started at the end of March 1966, when I had planned to get married in early March At this time I was playing good quality non-League football for Newbury Town in the Hellenic League against the likes of Chelsea A etc. I had been given the Saturday off before the wedding to prepare, however my local club who I had played for as a boy, South View from Basingstoke, asked me to turn out as a ringer for their reserve side. This I did without anyone knowing from my family, or wife to be. As is luck I suffered a serious fracture of both fibia and tibia just below the knee. To make it even worse it happened two minutes from the end. I lay on the stretcher in Basingstoke hospital while everyone tried to find my mum, dad, and fiancée. They eventually arrived at seven o'clock; you can imagine what followed.

I had already got my block of tickets for the World Cup and I was further distraught by the thought of missing the club tour at Easter to Belgium and Holland. I had at this stage not thought through what Newbury were about to say. Needless to say the wedding was postponed for six weeks. I got married in a full leg plaster and crutches. My suit trousers were split and kept together with safety pins. Needless to say further I missed the tour and Newbury cancelled my contract. Having said all this it appeared to me the most important thing was to set my sights on Wembley. My leg was responding reasonably well but in the end it was to be October before the full plaster came off!

About a week before the first game I realised that I needed to work out how I was going to get to Wembley and White City. I was by now being offered considerable bribes to sell my tickets. This is where a friend came into play,

Roger Barker (if you ever read this Roger please contact me, we lost contact some thirty years ago) who had just bought an MG Midget sports car. Roger's father was the local milkman and Roger had driven milk floats around the yard since about eight so I was supremely confident about Roger's ability to get us to the games. Fortunately the top was a convertible so it became apparent as I was 6' and could not bend my leg we would have to go to every game with the hood down and my leg out on the front of the car, resting on the windscreen. I do not think the Police would allow it now but in '66 the local bobby still existed and much policing was done with good spirit and common sense. The opening game arrived – would this work or not?

Ramsay's outburst against the Argentinians did not go down to well in South America.

We set off from Basing on what is now the A30 and then was the main road to London. As we had already worked out, we were bound to attract attention so why not go the whole hog. The local paper saw us off to the first game, my white plaster cast wrapped in a Union Jack with flags all over the car. We were tooting all the way and at Sunningdale Railway crossing someone even signed his name on my plaster. Needless to say we had a wonderful journey up and at every traffic light became the centre of attraction. Trying to park in Wembley car park was in itself a nightmare trying to keep the leg from being knocked. The next major job for Roger was to get me out of the car. This was accomplished and with crutches swinging we headed off for our block which turned out to be immediately behind the goal over the entrance tunnel. In those days your block of tickets was for the same area. By the end of the tournament the whole of the section looked for my arrival and I received great cheers when I arrived. Needless to say I did not miss one game at White City or Wembley.

Roger was a great companion and in a stranger sort of way was like my personal assistant helping me in every way (except when I went to the toilet). Everything was memorable. I moved around on one leg like a circus turn. I think the World Cup was a marvellous parade of fun and good humour.

There were moments for me I will never forget in addition to seeing England hold the World Cup aloft as winners. I am fifty-six now, in those days I was twenty-one and felt the cup was ours to keep. How wrong, and will I ever see England as winners again in my lifetime? I very much doubt it. The Geoff Hurst disputed goal, from where I was behind the goal, it was at least a foot over. The sending-off of Ratin from Argentina, the confrontation between Nobby Stiles and Perfumo of Argentina. The leaving out of Jimmy Greaves, Bobby Charlton's goal, and perhaps seeing Eusebio at his best were all great memories.

But one incident will always remain in my mind forever and that was looking up at the scoreboard during the England *v.* Argentina game and seeing the score North Korea 3 Portugal 0. As we all know the Portuguese got their act together and won 5-3. For a brief moment the whole stadium went quiet, whether the players on the pitch noticed I don't know, and then broke out into thunderous applause of disbelief. It was a memorable and lasting tournament, which will live with me all my life.

The way home from the final took five hours to do 50 miles, such was the excitement on the streets. When we got home in the early hours of the morning my wife was at my parents' house. Perhaps I should have realised at that moment of time football did and still does dictate my life. I now watch in sunnier climes in Malta where I have chosen to retire, but a visit back to England sees me looking for the fixture list. I was lucky enough to go to Argentina in '78, alas England did not qualify. Now I will treat myself to Japan/Korea. Having worked for a Japanese company it will be nice to see how Japanese football has progressed. My lasting wish is to be able to watch the World Cup when it finally goes to Africa. I cannot imagine the excitement.

Bobby Charlton was the hero as England won a magnificent semi-final against Portugal.

For me there can never be a World Cup like '66 but who cares, the memories linger on. Football has given me many great moments and the nearest thing I experienced to '66 was the Atlanta Olympics in 1996.

P. Barber

I was fifteen years old at Purley Grammar school in 1966 and had been watching football since I was nine, mostly Crystal Palace and local amateur sides. My first Wembley game was the Amateur Cup final in 1963 between Wimbledon and Sutton. By 1966 I had still not been to a full international match at Wembley.

We started off with a four-match ticket in the interests of economy as we wanted seats rather than standing and also we didn't really think at that stage that England would go all the way. My first game was France v. Mexico and my first memory was the colourful nature of the Mexican fans, all very much in contrast to the standard 'grey' of the England fans. That game was on a Wednesday evening and in the afternoon we had had our school sports. I was in most events and during the game I got cramp being in the constricted seats at Wembley and not able to stretch my legs properly. In the event I thought that it was not much of a game and I remember at the time thinking that it was no better to watch than the amateur ones I was used to.

Next game was England v. Mexico on a Saturday night. There was a bit of tension about that night as we had drawn the opening game. The fans were ready to moan, especially at Roger Hunt perhaps because, unlike their London heroes such as Moore, Hurst and

Greaves, he was with a northern club. This too wasn't much of a game until Charlton brought it to life with his superb goal, which changed everything. I learned later that the linesman had his flag up to indicate that Greaves was in an offside position but the goal was given.

England *v.* France was on the following Wednesday. I remember this as a rough game; very physical with some bad tackles, especially from Stiles. It was not memorable for the football but for the result. I got back home very late but stayed up even later to put in all the details into my programme.

Then came England *v.* Argentina; one of my top ten games of all in my life of watching football – which has now taken in over four thousand games. It was a warm sunny afternoon and the buzz in the crowd was because there was now at last a feeling that just maybe we could go all the way. It was for this my first afternoon, daylight game that I really got the feel of Wembley Way thronged with fans and lined with souvenir sellers. It really was a tight match early on. Argentina looked really good and the game looked like developing into a classic. In the crowd we weren't really aware of all the niggles and shirt tugging that was going on and all the complaints to, and pressure on, the referee. Ratin seemed a giant of a figure, very much in command. When he was sent off there was a tremendous explosion of excitement in the crowd, it was such a rare occurrence in those days. After that it became surreal! The match was stopped for a long time to sort it all out and it looked as though the whole Argentinean team would go off in protest. Ratin had that long walk round back to the tunnel with the abuse of the fans ringing in his ears all the way. Even with him gone it was a hard game. One felt that Argentina could have scored at any time. With twenty minutes to go Peters crossed and Hurst scored. I have a vivid memory of the Argentine goalkeeper gesticulating wildly – was it to the referee or to his own defender?

Mighty Hungary crush champions

Brazil were eliminated from the tournament in the opening stages by Hungary.

Charlton (still airborne) crashes home an unstoppable second for England in the semi-final.

That was it for us. I don't recall being too devastated at not getting to the final games.

D. Barber

CHAPTER 3

The Final

The day of the final was very hot but rather showery. Television coverage began early that day and I began by watching that at home before setting off to the stadium with my 'lucky' routine. This day remains one of the great football occasions of my life.

The heavy showers and weather generally rather seemed to reflect England's performance on the day. I recall that there were quite a few German supporters around us in our section, with their national colours, even though the team played in black and white. I liked the fact that we were playing in red and have always felt that it suits us.

I got to the ground nice and early and I recall Moore leading out the teams. I'd seen him many times at West Ham. I was a fan of Peters, who Alf had said was twenty-five years ahead of his time with elegance and craft. I was not all that worried when we went a goal down on the basis that the side which scores first never wins in World Cup finals. It was good to see the equaliser go in at our end. There was a great deal of banter between rival fans but no rancour at this or any other game I went to. I reckon that when tickets are sold well in advance it usually means that the real fans are the ones who buy them.

England seemed out for a 2-1 win with only a minute or two to go but the man who was for me the outstanding German player of the tournament changed all that – for all Beckenbauer's class, it was Haller who was the star for me. Any team that concedes an equaliser so late on in a game has undoubtedly lost the psychological initiative. Both sides were very tired. I recall Alf getting the lads up on their feet.

When it came to the goal I recall the agony of waiting while the referee consulted the Russian linesman. It seemed like a week. When the referee turned to point to the centre spot I just turned and hugged the person next to me – I had no idea who it was. The sun was shining by the time Hurst got the fourth goal.

At the end there was the overwhelming feeling that you had really seen history being made. Football had lifted you out of your ordinary everyday life for a while. I already knew very well how special football was, but the World Cup tournament and this final in particular put it in a global perspective and gave a totally new dimension for me. I recall feeling a supreme pride in being English with all that is best about that.

D. Davies

The WORLD CUP FINAL

on Saturday will be the greatest Soccer game ever staged in Britain.

Left: *A media forecast before the match.* Right: *The banner presented to Bobby Moore by the West German captain.*

Watching the final on the television was agony. We had relatives over from Canada and they couldn't understand what all the fuss was about. I ended up sitting on the living room floor because we didn't have enough chairs. I thought of my friend who happened to be sailing in his dinghy off the Devon coast that day. He listened to the radio commentary out at sea. I have one personal observation about the final and that concerns whether or not Hunt was inhibited by the crowd. When the ball came down from the bar could he not so easily have just tapped it in to make sure as he would certainly have done at Liverpool.

This, I would say, was the first time football was important to the nation as a whole. I went to the FA straight from A levels aged nineteen and in my first week was acting as interpreter for a visiting German under 23 side. Alf Ramsay had his office nearby where I was working and I used to take him his tea. He was a very serene man. He had a dry sense of humour. He got on very well with players as he was very good at taking the piss nicely. It was obvious that they loved him.

D. Barber

Being at the 'wrong end' at the final I can throw no further light on Hurst's

A ticket for the standing area opposite the players' tunnel for the World Cup final of 30 July 1966.

disputed goal in extra time. I have never yet been completely convinced that the ball was over the line. There was, however, no doubt about the last one which rocketed in to the net below me and which I shall never forget.

There was one last event which sticks in my memory. It occurred at about 10.30 p.m. on the night of the final when we were banned from the local pub for insisting that everyone in the establishment join in community singing of the World Cup victory anthems (I was readmitted the following day on compassionate grounds).

Probably my most valued possession is my copy of the composite official souvenir programme which listed all the tournament matches, nationwide. When it was all over I spent hours taking it apart and typing in every players' name, official, goalscorer, attendance, sendings off etc. I doubt if there is a more compact record in existence. The crowning moment came some months after the end of the tournament when, with my young son, I spent a couple of hours with the England team at the Banks' training ground at Ealing and all the World Cup players who were there autographed the programme for me. I remember that dear old Bobby Moore told me he had never seen a programme like it and spent quite a long time browsing through it.

J. Collier

I attended all the London games during the 1966 World Cup. I still have my match tickets and programmes and other souvenirs like teatowel and handkerchief and replica (broken) of the Jules Rimet trophy. I was with two teacher colleagues at the World Cup final but they had to leave before the extra time, unaware that their train had been held back to allow for it. I stayed on because I was soon to be going to the Cassius Clay v. Brian London World Heavyweight title fight.

I remember little in real detail about the games other than Ratin being sent off and the fact that I didn't hear one swearword at any of the games. I take great pride in having been there. After the final I stayed on in London for another week or so for the big title fight – Cassius Clay signed my World Cup ticket stub.

D. Parkinson

For the final, Dad moved all the furniture and placed the television in the centre of the room and we all said what are you doing that for. His reply was, 'It's going to be worth watching, I just know it is'. The last time we had heard him say that was before the Eintracht Frankfurt v. Real Madrid game – say no more!

When England scored those goals it was history in the making. The whole of Milton Avenue ran out into the street

The England mascot being photographed outside Wembley by visiting fans.

Jimmy Greaves, who played in the early games, was injured and missed the final. His replacement, Geoff Hurst, scored a hat-trick.

shouting 'England, England'! For me, after the sixties and possibly a few games in the seventies, it's never been the same .

A. Bell

It was such an awful feeling to have victory snatched away. Playing conditions were good. It had been raining and the ball moved around well even if it was a bit on the heavy side. We were fitter and came on more and more – I felt we were getting more room in extra time. I was about four yards out, marked by Weber under the German man-to-man marking system, which I had experienced before playing against Cologne. I thought that the ball had gone into the roof of the net. I was totally convinced it was over the line. I'd have loved to get on the score sheet in the final but it all happened so quickly and I just took it as a goal that had been scored. When the uncertainty arose a few players from both sides went over to the line to make our points. I was one of them.

Afterwards most of it is largely a blur; the celebrations in the dressing room and so on. The journey back to Hendon Hall Hotel was fantastic with so much celebration all the way. Then we came back in to the Royal Garden and the four teams that had reached the semi-final stage had a joint banquet. That was very memorable. It was impossible to get out after that as there were no taxis and the place was surrounded. I didn't go on anywhere afterwards.

When it was all over I remember feeling a tremendous kind of relief that after all the build up and all the games themselves we had finally done it.

Roger Hunt

I am a life-long Liverpool supporter. On the day before the World Cup final in 1966 I got a ticket for the game because my brother just happened to pick one up that was going for sale in a local pub. In the event I never went to the game because I couldn't find anyone to go with at such short notice and I didn't want to go down on my own. I still have the ticket, complete and unused.

I watched the final on the television and remember being struck when a camera zoomed in on a banner which read 'Next to Liverpool, England are the Greatest'. I thought, 'I could have been there' and regretted it. I had been to all the games at Goodison Park.

T. Higham

After the semi-final I remember a good quote from the Portugal manager who, when he was asked who he thought would win the World Cup final, replied, 'We've just seen it haven't we?' Greaves was not fit but if he had been fit by the time of the final would they have changed the team? With England's third goal Roger Hunt was absolutely certain that the ball was over the line; that it had crossed the line while in the air.

Towards the end of extra time I noticed that the referee did have his whistle in his mouth. I thought he was going to blow. Just five people or so were trying to get onto the pitch. I have since spoken to one of them. He was only eighteen then. He thought the referee was about to blow. He ran straight into the arms of a policeman who put him back into the crowd so he missed the goal.

Kenneth Wolstenholme

The final is now rather a blur of emotions. I recall Jack Charlton giving away the free kick from which Germany equalised, and Nobby Stiles' celebrations afterwards. At school at the end of term the

The most famous commentary quotation of all time.

atmosphere had been terrific and once we all got back in September the final was the only topic of conversation.

I. Dix

At Wembley I was behind the goal-line about midway between the goal and the corner flag to the right at the end where Hurst scored England's controversial third goal. In terms of quality the game was perhaps not all that special, but the atmosphere and the drama more than compensated. My special recollections are the resemblance of Helmut Haller to Albert Quixall and England's equaliser – perfectly placed free kick from Moore, perfectly judged header from Hurst, which was reminiscent of the Eusebio/Torres partnership against Hungary.

There was also Jack Charlton's foul leading to Germany's equaliser. As I saw it, the German forward was obstructing him from getting to a high dropping ball and I hoped he would have the sense to leave it and appeal for obstruction. Instead, of course, he went for the ball, gave away a free kick and in the resulting scramble Weber equalised.

I didn't think that Hurst's controversial goal was in but I wasn't in the best position to judge. The second period of extra time was very nerve wracking. Moore was very cool as he

The management lead out their teams for the 1966 World Cup final.

broke up West Germany's final attack and with everyone around me yelling at him to boot it up field he brought the ball out of defence and played it forward to Hurst to run on with and finish. Over all I still feel tremendously privileged to have been present at England's greatest football success and to have seen Eusebio and that marvellous Portugal team at their best.

After 1966 it was quite some time before I could enjoy watching professional football again. I had always been a Bury supporter although I couldn't watch them much due to my own playing commitments. In 1966/67 they were relegated from the old Second Division. Every time I saw them, Eusebio and his Portugal team mates would come to mind and I would think 'What am I

The teams lined up for the anthems.

Referee Dienst tosses up before the 1966 World Cup final at Wembley.

Emmerich fires a shot past Cohen and Peters.

doing watching this?' I eventually cured myself by comparing what I was watching at Gigg Lane favourably against the West Germany semi-final!

D. Roberts

The final was a wonderful but totally exhausting and draining experience. It was a very long day as I arrived early to find a good spot and sat down to rest with my sandwiches. The roar of the crowd and the constant chant of 'England! England!' reverberating around the magnificent stadium was deafening. I still remember the contrasting hush from the English supporters when the first German goal went in the net. There was no crowd segregation and a very large German had positioned himself right in front of me. I don't think he was drunk but he was certainly very, very excited by the whole occasion. He had a large German flag which he kept waving whenever either team looked like scoring – so I couldn't see much at all – and he kept shouting 'Uwe/England, England/Uwe' alternately (Uwe Seeler was Germany's captain). The tension was unbelievable, especially when Germany were awarded a hotly contested free kick on the stroke of ninety minutes and the ball ended up in the net. It was too much for me and I burst into tears! This was followed by the agonising wait for the referee's decision on the famous Hurst – did it cross the line or not – goal. That apart, extra time seemed to pass in a flash – suddenly it was all over and everyone was hugging everyone in sight. The actual presentation of the cup was too far away for me to really see, only the roar from the crowd gave me a clue as to what was happening. It was one of the few things better seen later on TV rather than actually being there. I just remember jumping up and down and cheering as the team ran past with the trophy and my hands stinging for ages afterwards from all the clapping.

Five days later it was my twenty-first birthday. My parents had booked a table at a dinner-dance restaurant and had a special cake made. No, it didn't have pretty pink icing but a football pitch with a miniature England team on it. As I cut into it in the time honoured fashion it was not the strains of *Twenty-one Today* that the band played but *When the Reds Come Marching In* – our unofficial England anthem for the World Cupfinal: a great occasion that I shall always be proud to have attended.

Mrs P. Chaston

In 1966 I was a thirteen year old schoolboy, mad about soccer and hoping against hope that England could win the World Cup. I covered every blade of grass with the team as I watched them make their black and white progress to the final on the family's Ultra Bermuda television set. I gloried in Bobby Charlton's imperious strike against Mexico, thrilled at Geoff Hurst's glancing header against the hard men of Argentina and winced as Nobby Stiles set about the marking of Eusebio.

Then onto the final against the other old enemy, West Germany; a match of nail-biting tension which had absolutely everything including the right result. The next morning I went out and bought every Sunday newspaper, removed the back pages and sellotaped them all into the World Cup Willy scrapbook – which I have to this day.

Best of all though was the moment when my hero Bobby Moore wiped his hands, leaned forward and accepted the Jules Rimet trophy from the Queen – football, as they were later to sing, had 'come home'. A wonderful time in a summer full of clichés and through it all the majesty of Wembley and the twin towers ascending over my own magical moment.
a

P.R. Stanton

Jack Charlton can do nothing about it!

Haller scores Germany's first goal.

Hurst equalises after 18 minutes.

Peters gives England a 2-1 lead.

As a Londoner and Arsenal supporter I have had the good fortune to experience many visits to Wembley. There were the less memorable moments, such as against Swindon, as well as the wins against Manchester United in 1979 and, of course, the 1971 double-achieving win against Liverpool (after winning the League title at Tottenham!)

My first memories of going to Wembley will be of 1966. My father had bought two season tickets for all the England World Cup games. We watched every one – all but one being at Wembley. The final itself had an unreal atmosphere. There was obviously great support for England but all around us were seated overseas visitors. Perhaps our surname had confused those allocating the tickets. Our companions were a little more reserved than my father and me – we were England supporters before Norman Tebbit invented the test.

I missed Hurst's last goal and the presentations as I had to leave before the end. Extra-time had made me late to meet my girlfriend and her parents who I was joining to go on holiday. I did not have the nerve to miss the train. I would now. However, it was still an unforgettable introduction to Wembley and the feeling of 'being there' will always be with me.

P. di Giuseppe

I've already bored many of the nation on the documentary which was first shown in 1996. Aged just seventeen, I was running towards the Wembley pitch on July 30th when I saw Hurst heading towards the penalty area, just before the end of extra time. I crouched down not far from the cameramen. Probably only four spectators were closer to the bulging net than I was. I remember how sporting the German fans were in defeat (those were the days!) and (perhaps controversially) feeling that the Germans deserved to take it to extra time. I also went to the White City match and to Spain *v.* West Germany at Villa Park. I was also at matches on consecutive Saturdays when I witnessed the then very unusual event of a sending off (both Argentinians), one versus West Germany, the other at Wembley! I was very, very lucky to obtain a final ticket at the last minute when friend who had been drawn out in the ballot and who didn't want to cancel his holiday offered it to me. I smashed a window in our back garden trying to emulate Charlton's famous long-range strike the evening after he netted with it. I missed Hurst's goal against Argentina as I was pointing out the change on the Wembley scoreboard which recorded the stages of Portugal's sensational recovery to beat the Koreans: 5-3 after even more sensationally trailing 3-0. I remember losing over half my week's wages to a colleague who had taken up my none-too-generous odds of 20-1 against Korea qualifying for the quarter-finals – a mean thing to do to a seventeen year old. I remember seeing photos of two very miserable looking Englishmen straight after England had won the Cup. They were, of course, those two Dagenham lads, Ramsey and Greaves.

A. Howland

Eventually, of course, England met Germany in the final. The night before the game I was in a restaurant with my then girlfriend, having a meal, when I noticed a German couple in the restaurant, they

Peters' goal from another angle.

clearly couldn't speak English and I couldn't speak German but on passing their table I turned to them, signalling with my fingers and said Germany two England four. They understood, shook their heads and there was much amiable laughter and back slapping. They indicated they were going to Wembley the next day. I often wonder whether they ever recalled the incident as things turned out. The major incident in the cup final was, of course the ball off the crossbar and that wonderful Russian linesman. We were actually behind that goal and to the side of the goal towards that linesman. When the incident happened it happened so fast that we all turned to each other and said 'Did it go in?' If we were all honest we have to say that there was no way of telling. When the linesman gave the goal we were ecstatic but we must confess that afterwards we did wonder whether or not it was the influence of the home crowd that persuaded him. In all honesty I cannot see how he could tell. As far as we were concerned we were pleased to see the last of Geoff Hurst's goals scored because it removed the controversy. Germany were, of course, pressing forward for an equaliser and this left them open at the back. I still believe therefore, that that was the defining moment in the game and I still wonder whether England won it with true merit. That said, and on balance, I believe the crowd felt that they did. Particularly as Germany's late equalizer in normal time was so distressing – we were all looking at our watches willing the referee to blow and that equalising goal was like being kicked in the belt.

My final memory must be London during the evening of the actual final. Earlier in the competition I had been in Leicester Square leaning against some railings, waiting for my friends, when I suddenly realised I was looking at a coach stuck in the traffic. There looking at me was Bobby Moore and other England players, they had taken time out to go to the cinema. The film they actually went to see was, perhaps, prophetic as it was called *The Red Baron*, the First World War film about the flying aces. There was considerable excitement in Leicester Square when it was realised who was there. This, however, was nothing like the excitement in and around the major sites of London that evening. It was all good-natured stuff and the various nationalities joined in, in what can only be described in those days as football comradeship. We actually went to see a show. The whole show was distracted because the noise from out in the street was deafening. The horns beeping the chant could be clearly heard and if the truth was known we all wanted to get out of the theatre and join the excitement. A memorable two weeks, which I shall never ever forget.

K. Metcalfe

A child of the sixties, I was eighteen, having just done my A levels and living in a Lancashire mill town. I had secured a series of tickets following the instructions set out in a newspaper article. An embryo entrepreneur, I sold them off, but retained the ticket for the final. I worked all night on the Friday in the local mill, nicked off early and caught the first train out of Colne for London.

You need to understand that I had never been to London on my own before and the train fare of £5 return was a lot of money to me. I had an incredible day and would be pleased to write you an account of it. I got lost. I got cramp on the train. I met Edward Heath who signed my programme over the Queen's face. I stood behind the goal where the controversial goal was scored. I survived the entire day on a bar of chocolate. I saw Cassius Clay (as he then was) and Harold Wilson. Walking down Wembley Way on the way out, the Portuguese team coach stopped in the traffic, a player opened the window

The heart-stopping last minute equaliser by Weber. Was there a handball?

and pointing to the England rosette on the jacket of the fan next to me, he removed his gold-tie pin and we swapped them. I arrived back in Colne at midnight.

G. Holehouse

The most interesting events in the final have been shown many times on television. I can remember being concerned at how good the German team was, and was realising pretty quickly that it was going to be a struggle to beat them. I can remember being impressed by the boundless energy of Alan Ball who covered prodigious areas of the pitch, and being annoyed at a group of young German supporters standing next to us who continuously blew their hunting horns. We gave a very big cheer when our favourite Russian linesman, who was close to where we were standing, gave England's goal.

I cannot remember there being as much hype in the media as there is nowadays but I suppose there was, and the spectators from the different countries were not segregated as far as I can remember. I still have my Official Souvenir Programme and my Wembley Final Ticket and Final Programme.

R. Beswick

I noticed an advert in the *Evening Standard* on the Thursday evening advertising tickets for sale. If my memory serves me well it was a £1 10/- ticket on sale for £4. I absconded from my job at Heathrow for a three hour lunch on the Friday to go and purchase three tickets for my two workmates and myself. I am no longer in contact with either but after lunch at Ruislip Manor at one of the guys' houses we proceeded to Wembley by car. It was a VW Beetle. We had our Union Jacks proudly flying from the windows of the car but we got jibes about the make of the car when we stopped at traffic lights. It was both of the guys' first football game, and for one of them, the last (I think). I had been going to Chelsea since 1955 and still do. The other chap went to Chelsea for about four years

German euphoria following the equaliser.

after 1966 but then I never saw him again.

Amazingly, when I was in hospital in 1970 with a broken leg, my girlfriend brought me a football magazine – I think it was *Charles Buchan Football Monthly* – and there was an article about the 1970 World Cup final. I opened the first page and there was quite a close-up view of the crowd from '66 and there was the three of us clearly seen waving our Union Jacks! I kept the magazine for about eight years but unfortunately my wife threw it out!

For the game I was directly behind the goal where the controversy occurred. I clearly remember Roger Hunt wheeling away without attempting to make an effort to put the ball over the line, believing it to be over. That was it apart from the evening – when I met this Polish girl but I won't go into that – which rounded off a memorable day.

V. Pierce

England had it all to do again.

What happened between the end of ninety minutes and the start of extra time is more personal, more connected with the passion of the event, which carried away a nation.

Germany, West Germany as then was, had just equalized, remember. We had been minutes away from victory, now it had to be done all over again. The looks on the faces around me were anxious, drawn and there was silence over which the occasional curse or question could be heard. Then, quite without embarrassment, a well-dressed man of middle years, a row in front of me, dropped to his knees, bowed his head, raised his hands in prayer and said, quite plainly: 'God, please, you can not let us lose to the bloody Germans'. He looked much happier when he got up and we all felt a bit better because he had done openly what all of us must have been doing silently; I know I was. Silly, isn't it, to get so emotional about a game.

But that night, I was supposed to attend the official banquet at the Royal Garden Hotel. My wife and I were caught up in the massed crowds a half mile away and never got there; and never regretted it, so wonderful was it to be among so many people, so deliriously happy. It would be nice to be alive when it comes back to this country and go through it all again; although, for heaven's sake, not with extra time.

C. Toye

England prepare themselves to go and beat Germany for the second time.

We married in September 1965. Even though we were, and still are, fervent Fulham fans and Eric had regularly attended international matches, there was no way we ever thought of buying a ticket for any of the World Cup games. We didn't even own a television!

We watched the final on my parents' TV in their home, Wardo Avenue, Fulham. After the cup had been presented to Bobby Moore, mention was made of the team travelling to a reception at the Royal Garden Hotel, Kensington. We decided to go there, and travelled by public transport. It was easy to find a standing position outside The Goat. Cars travelling past the hotel hooted da da da-da-da da-da-da-da. Eventually police stopped the traffic. The team arrived by coach. The cheers were tremendous. We had an excellent view of the team, as they stood in front of the hotel. Bobby Moore held the cup high. We were so proud!

We took the tube back to Putney Bridge Station, to go to our regular Saturday night haunt, The Golden Lion, Fulham High Street, then home of the Fulham Supporters Club. George

Cohen's mum was sitting on a stool in the far corner of the saloon bar, talking to Anne Barron, wife of Jack, the licensee. Mrs Cohen was there by invitation of the Barrons. Anne spent much of the evening talking to her. It was a party night!

It was all so simple. Every person encountered that evening was happy and well-behaved. It was so easy to get in position outside the hotel. But, despite re-running videos of the scene, I've never been able to 'find' us in the crowd, although The Goat is easily identifiable.

Mrs M. Greenwood

I was there at the final (block A22) and I still have my ten shilling ticket, programme and rosette. I took some photographs at the game but I was a long way behind the goal so they are not brilliant but they mean a lot to me.

I walked home after the game to my parents' house in Shepherd's Bush, had a sandwich and then joined in the celebrations at a local pub. I did not take off my rosette until the following Wednesday. This caused consternation from my then new employers Barclays Bank but I refused to remove it. The staff canteen was in the head office of Barclays Bank Limited and the other staff bet me I would not wear it for lunch as it would mean going past the directors' dining room. I kept it on and was duly spotted by one of the hierarchy and summoned into their dining room. He asked me to tell the board all about the match. I had been in the job only three weeks and was already having a drink with

Was it finally over?

the board!

I attended all the London games. I have a copy of the *FA World Cup Report*, which I browse through now and again. July 30th was an unforgettable day for me. It is not often you can really say of something important, 'I was there'.

Last season 'I was there' when Jimmy Glass scored the goal that kept Carlisle in the League. I wonder if anyone else has achieved such an unusual 'double'?

K. Porter

I was twenty-three years old in 1966 when the World Cup was staged at Wembley. Having been injured at the age of nineteen whilst playing football, I was an eager spectator of the sport and was, and still am, an avid Chelsea supporter.

My wife Pat, then my fiancée, was working for a large company. Her close friend worked in the travel department of the same company and asked Pat if she thought I would be interested in two free tickets for the World Cup. Would I be interested? I jumped at the chance. However, it was the ninth person I asked – a work colleague some years older than myself – who finally accepted my invitation to join me at Wembley. It was inconceivable to me that people were refusing a free ticket to such a prestigious event, but it appeared that many people had organised their own parties at home or in clubs in order to watch the big match. If necessary I would have gone alone and given the ticket away when I got to the ground. It was one event that I was determined not to miss and to this day it remains one of the major high spots in my life. Our tickets were for use within the

DC Jones felt a goal was coming and snapped this just as Hurst's shot was coming down off the crossbar.

Hurst puts the game beyond doubt with England's fourth goal.

German contingent of supporters, which obviously concerned us a little. Our fears were groundless. The German fans had come well prepared with bags and holdalls full of beer and spirits which they generously shared with us throughout the match and as the final whistle blew several German fans shared in our obvious elation by hugging us and shaking us by the hand. I felt immensely proud and privileged to be at Wembley on that memorable day. I don't think the girl who offered me the tickets will ever really know the depth of my gratitude.

M. Marks

I have been with Bromsgrove Rovers for over fifty years and attended the World Cup final with a colleague. We were behind the goal where Geoff Hurst scored to win the game.

We had a special train journey from Birmingham Snow Hill direct to Wembley with dinner on the return journey. Due to extra time the train left without us and we had to return by ordinary train via London. On arriving back at Birmingham I refused to give my ticket up as I was going to complain, and after a lot of argument I retained the ticket and was eventually reimbursed by British Rail. I still have the ticket, which I believe is the only one in existence.

C. Poole

In 1966 I had a ticket for the games in the North West. I got a ticket for the Everton FA Cup final and entered a draw for a ticket for the World Cup final. I remember getting a phone message from my dad saying I'd been lucky and had drawn one but it had to be accepted within two hours so my dad did it all for me. It was marvellous to go to two finals in one year.

I saw the Koreans go three goals up and the local crowd really backed them as they had no fans of their own. It could never be the same again even if we had got 2006. Fans were so much more friendly in those days.

I. Biggins

In January 1966 I sent for a ten-match ticket. I went to the games at Old Trafford and one at Everton and gave the rest away to friends.

For the World Cup final we were outside Wembley at 12.30 waiting for the ground to open at 1.00. We found ourselves on the barrier which was overlooking the players' tunnel. After the game I remember seeing Alan Ball and Nobby Stiles swap shirts. We were staying in Edgeware. We bumped into some very blonde Germans who were friendly and with whom we swapped flags. I remember the English fans singing, 'We won the war'.

I remember entering a *Daily Express* competition to win an England team photo signed by all the players. I ended up with a runners-up prize, which was a copy of that, which I still have framed and up on my wall.

G. Kay

In 1966 I was working at the Royal School for the Deaf in Exeter and I took it upon myself to organise a summer outing to Hope Cove without at

It is all over now!

The England bench in ecstacy – apart from a stunned Ramsay.

the time realising it would clash with the World Cup final. On the actual day we borrowed a twelve inch portable television and powered it with two car batteries. Then we all watched the final in a tent in the middle of the field. When we got back to the school we learned that there had been a power cut there and no one who had been on the premises that day had been able to watch the final at all!

Derek

My second son was a chorister at Exeter Cathedral and he was due to be confirmed in the Cathedral on the afternoon of Saturday 30th July 1966. We all travelled down from South Devon for this important service. Bishop Mercer was an eccentric gentleman. He had forgotten all about the confirmation until someone went to find him in front of his television where he had settled down to watch the World Cup final. After that he was kept in touch by the Dean during the service and afterwards he did not join the parents for tea as was always the normal practice on such occasions but went off straight back to his television for the rest of the game.

Mrs M. Ridge

In 1966 I was just ten years old and on Saturday 30th July I went on a coach outing with my cub pack from Leicestershire to London. It was my first ever journey on a motorway. Going down we were singing the World Cup Willie song and the motorway was packed with coaches going to the final. We went to Earls Court for the Royal Tournament. There was no news at all about the final until the actual result was announced upon which there was

Nobby Stiles is overjoyed at the result.

enormous cheering and the whole place emptied. This was one of my very first memories of the 'real world' from childhood.

D. Rogers

My wife and I were at Fontainbleu while England's team were winning the World Cup; and at the Folies Bergere in the evening – a cheerful and memorable occasion indeed!

S. Downing

I have always hated football and everything about it and only ever went to Anfield twice in my life, despite coming from a football mad family.

We all sat round the television to watch the final and afterwards my brother went out with his girlfriend to celebrate England being World Champions. On the way back, at 11.30 p.m., a time we all remember exactly like the Kennedy assassination, they were both knocked down by a hit and run driver. My brother pulled his girlfriend out of the way as best he could so she was less badly hurt. He was in hospital for months after that and even now all these years later he still walks with a limp.

Mrs S. Jones

In Guernsey on the day of the World Cup final in 1966 absolutely everywhere was deserted. All the newspapers arrived on the island late that day and had to be delivered so I drove and walked all over doing my belated deliveries and thus missed the game as there were, of course, no such things as 'walkmans' in those days. The whole place was like a ghost town.

S. Harney

In 1966 I had a season ticket for every game culminating in the final. The friend that had attended every match with me was always late which meant we never got to see the kick-off. For the final I insisted that we would go separately as I was looking forward to the pre-match entertainment and the build up of atmosphere and was determined not to miss the kick-off at the biggest match of the whole lot. He assured me he was travelling down to Wembley the day before, to make sure he would be on time as he felt that, as a Jew, he could make a protest by not standing up for the German national anthem. Unfortunately for him he was late yet again and missed the opportunity to make his protest, and the kick off! As a Scotsman I had mixed feelings when England won!

C. Muir

Saturday July 30th saw me, with my family, marooned in a boarding house in Scarborough for the annual holiday fortnight. As a twelve-year-old boy, already football daft, I took along my unfinished World Cup Willie scrapbook and my most treasured possession, a hand knitted black and amber scarf that I had worn throughout the previous season when my team, Hull City, romped away with the Third Division title.

The morning was spent seeking a television set as our holiday abode only had radio. In those (almost Victorian) days public houses refused to allow minors on the premises so this task was indeed a very serious problem. Uncle Ted, the most convincing cockney spiv you could ever wish to meet that wasn't actually a cockney, came up trumps very, very late on with a one day family pass for a backstreet British Legion Club.

In we sneaked, being careful not to sit in someone's chair, into what was probably the biggest crowd they had had since VE day. The actual television set was, of course,

Gordon Banks celebrates the win.

Bobby Charlton in tears of victory.

black and white, had about a 12" screen, and positioned high up on a wall above a bingo caller. The atmosphere was wonderful – like Christmas Eve – until I put a sixpence into the one-armed bandit. Bells rang and lights flashed and up popped a winning run and an absolute avalanche of silver sixpences flooded onto the floor. This caused a near riot. Firstly, I wasn't a member and secondly, as a twelve year old boy I should not even have been on the machine in the first place. As it was I had won the jackpot.

Uncle Ted, ever the peacemaker and craftily picking up as many of the sixpences as he could, tried to smooth the situation which was threatening to get out of hand and place our very presence in the club in jeopardy at a crucial time. The game was due to kick off shortly but the members were irate at this snotty nosed kid who had come from nowhere and won their jackpot. In the end a compromise was reached. I was allowed to keep £1 and somehow, so too was my cousin, Uncle Ted's own son. What happened to the rest, still spread out over the floor, I will never know. I felt like one of the great train robbers huddled in a corner trying to watch the final through a haze of woodbine smoke and muttered threats. So bad was the feeling towards our party that Uncle Ted whisked us out of the place the minute the final whistle blew with the game undecided and the score agonisingly equalised.

Back at the boarding house tea was already being taken in silence. Whilst every other person in Britain was tuned into extra time in the World Cup final, I sat shamefaced in front of a cold meat salad feeling as though I had robbed someone. The only way I knew a goal had been scored was through a muffled cheer from nearby board and lodgings not so refined as ours!

G. Clark

Your season ticket book number was placed in a draw for a ticket for the final and a letter arrived at my house saying that we had been allocated just the one ticket only for the final at Wembley. Thomas and I tossed up for it and I was successful.

Tommy attended the semi-final match between West Germany and Russia. The match was of no importance to me other than to see the great Russian goalkeeper Lev Yashin who played in all black, and Franz Beckenbauer playing for Germany; one player in the autumn of his career and Beckenbauer in the spring of his. We all know what Beckenbauer contributed to world football at all levels afterwards.

I attended the World Cup Final with a friend of mine called Raymond, in days of travel when the coach left St John's Lane at midnight and pulled into the Wembley coach park at approximately six in the morning. I recall buying pints of milk from a milkman as he was going round on his float delivering to houses.

We all know what happened in the match. One of my memories after the game was the German supporters giving us bottles of beer which they had with them. I also remember their up to date buses with compartments at the side for luggage as opposed to the sort we had with the big boot at the back.

My first visit to Wembley was also in 1966 to see Everton *v.* Sheffield Wednesday in the Cup Final, so you can see I have very happy memories of 1966.

A. McDonald

I went to all the London games in 1966 and all my tickets for Wembley were in the same block, behind the goal where the controversial goal was. I have seen lots of World Cup finals from 1958 onwards but the one in England was obviously the best. I was asked by the BBC in 1998 to appear in a documentary on the World Cup because

Nobby Stiles and Jimmy Greaves hug each other after the victory.

of my having been to Sweden in 1958.

On the day of the final I took the train from Marylebone, which stopped at a station platform just behind turnstile block A. After the game eight total strangers including myself got into a compartment on the train back and one produced a full bottle of whiskey. Before the train reached Marylebone it had all gone.

I went out in Brighton that evening and everyone was elated with car horns hooting everywhere. I have kept lots of souvenirs from 1966.

M. Webster

Saturday July 30th 1966 was my wedding day! The wedding had of course been fixed up a very great deal earlier, long before anyone could have known who would be playing in the World Cup final. I suppose we could have tried to change it but we decided not to. It was timed for 3.00 p.m. and in the event it must have been one of the quickest weddings on record as even the vicar was very keen to get on with it and then watch the match. Half the men who had been invited didn't come at all or came on later. Lots of those who did come kept popping out to listen to the wireless. Even the reception was delayed because of the extra time but eventually, once England had won, everything was jubilant.

My fiancee himself was a football fan but he couldn't afford to go to the games live and had to follow them on the television.

Mrs P. Higgins

I went to all the North East group games then down to London for the last games including the final. At the final I was stood behind the goal at the end opposite the players' tunnel. That part of the ground seemed to have a lot of people in it from the North East, including one lady from Stockton-on-Tees who was so upset by the German equaliser that she sat down on the terraces and refused to watch the extra time. People around her fed her the information about how it was all going and only when we were 4-2 up would she get up and believe we had actually made it!

I was amazed at how many supporters the Germans had at the final. I also noticed that people's perceptions varied a lot between those who saw it on the TV and those who were actually there. My view is that Ball and Stiles were the two best players, a view not shared by all those with whom I have discussed it but who only saw it on the TV.

I drove back up the A1 afterwards. There was a huge volume of traffic with horns blazing and flags waving all the way.

D. Boag

I saw the group matches in the London area but my tickets ran out after the quarter-final against Argentina. I paid £5 to get a ticket for the final and went down with a pal. We stayed within a stone's throw from the ground in a working-class bed and breakfast. The landlady couldn't have been more friendly or nice. The workers who were lodging there were also very friendly.

I remember taking a loud horn to blow, which annoyed the nearby fans. I don't think Wembley was full. I went to a local pub after the game and had a fantastic

Bobby Moore recieves his medal from HRH Queen Elizabeth II.

evening. People from the B&B turned up and joined in and we all had a really fantastic party night.

P. Bradley

I well remember 1966 and all that. As Middlesbrough supporters we had all decided to adopt the North Korean team who beat Italy at Ayresome Park with a goal by Pak Do Ik. I bought a ticket for £6.50, which I used to see all the matches at Ayresome Park and Roker Park, and also the last three at Wembley. The final did not see a full house, there being less than the usual 100,000 there for it.

It was the greatest day of the century when my friend and I stood behind the goal where Geoff Hurst scored that final goal. We partied all night in the West End, caught the tube to Stanmore and I then drove home up the A1. I arrived home at 6.00 a.m. and didn't feel tired cos I was so elated by the whole thing. I didn't bother going to bed.

S. Denham

My mother had been born in Tottenham, North London, and had always been a fanatical Spurs supporter. One of my own earliest childhood

Moore, with the trophy, closely followed by hat-trick hero Hurst.

memories is of the day in 1961 when the Tottenham Hotspur football team travelled through the streets on an open topped bus to display the FA Cup and League trophies, having just achieved the 'double'. I was six years old and sat on my father's shoulders to see the bus go by and to cheer on our team. My interest in football was, therefore, well established by the time England hosted the World Cup in 1966 and I remember the final clearly. My mother and I found the tension of the extra time so unbearable that we had to leave the room where the television was and went to sit on the stairs outside. We put our hands over our ears so we could not hear what was happening either, but had given my father strict instructions to let us know if England scored. So we actually didn't see the goals as they happened or hear Kenneth Wolstenholme's legendary words, but we didn't care. It was enough that England won. These days, I manage to cope with the stresses of extra time, but penalty shoot-outs see me back on the stairs.

Gill Haynes

In 1966 my parents had saved up to take myself, my brother Gordon and my uncle on a two week, two centre holiday in Switzerland. The first week was to be in central Switzerland and was to be a chance for Gordon to show us places around Lake Luzern, which he had visited the previous year on a school trip. However, Gordon was taken ill with rheumatic fever so, rather than us all miss out on the holiday, my eldest brother, Paul, took Gordon's place. We left

Gordon in St Peter's Hospital, Chertsey while we went on holiday. The daily hospital routine involved blood pressure monitoring, pulse measurements, etc every six hours. During his several weeks in hospital, Gordon's pulse reached a record low during the World Cup final, which was on the television in his ward...which just goes to show that not everyone finds that football excites them to 'fever pitch'!

Jeff Haynes

My brother-in-law had managed to get two ten-match tickets and I went to just two of the games; the semi-final against Portugal and the final itself. I was only seventeen at the time and more interested in amateur football, both in terms of playing and watching and my memories of the World Cup are a bit of a blur. I do remember wearing a suit with a collar and tie, and that a lot of people dressed much more smartly in those days.

I went with my brother-in-law and we were at the players' tunnel end. He drove us from Hayes and we parked at a tube station and finished the journey by tube. I was very agitated by the game going to extra time because we had something to go on to that evening and so we had to dash away the minute it was over.

M. Baker

On the day of the final I actually locked up the White City just after 2.00 p.m.. I had a 'pass all barriers' card for Wembley itself so no problems about getting in.

I recall people almost crying when Germany equalised, yet my own worries at that moment concerned the possibility of a replay as the necessary arrangements were not exactly in place! I remember looking straight to the linesman for the third goal and seeing him point to the middle so I thought the goal would certainly be given.

A. Williams

I went to every one of the games played in London having obtained a ten-match ticket in the January before the games. I felt it was very cheap even for the time.

Until the quarter-finals I thought the games were pretty boring as such, even though they had atmosphere if England were playing. The journalists wanted

Inspirational captain Moore kisses the trophy.

Greaves to play and liven it up a bit. It came alive by the quarter-final. Argentina played well and forced us to lift our game. The semi against Portugal was the best game in the tournament. It was Bobby Charlton's best game and for me confirmed Eusebio as the player of the tournament.

On the day of the final I remember I wore a suit and tie, as many people did in those days for an occasion. I was at the players' tunnel end where the disputed goal was scored. I was a Chelsea fan, but lots of my friends who were Chelsea fans had not bothered getting tickets. I found myself surrounded by Liverpool fans. We could not see why the ref needed to consult the linesman as the ball looked so far over the goal line from our angle. The scousers made the point that if Hunt had been in any doubt he would have put the ball into the net himself so therefore there can't have been any. We worried that the referee was not going to give the goal.

After the final I went to a friends' engagement party in Willesden and this turned into a celebration party for the World Cup. His new fiancée got a bit fed up with all the football songs. On my way to Willesden, on foot, I popped into a pub and it was very quiet. There was a German commiserating with an Irish barman in this Irish pub about the English. The German was more friendly towards me than the Irishman.

J. Ince

Nobby Stiles does a jig of delight as the trophy is paraded around the ground.

Moore and the trophy raised aloft in triumph.

I had bought a part season ticket in the interests of economy and thus did not have a ticket for the final itself. I was then just seventeen and had had a part-time job for some time working in the Empire Pool box office. I was on duty there on the actual morning of the final and at 11.30 a.m. that very day my boss gave me a ten shilling ticket for the World Cup final. Work finished at 12.30, so it was a quick lunch then off to the ground just across the way to wait for it to open. I was one of the very first people into the stadium. I ended up standing next to an Argentinian with whom I chatted happily enough until kick off, although he was very much supporting Germany in the game.

I lived in the Wembley area then and had walked to all the previous games. After the final I walked down with the crowds to Wembley Park Station, then on a bit further to the first pub past it – the Chequer I think it was called. There I celebrated with an increasing number of happy fans. We were all jumping up and down so much that the floor began to give way and the police were called and they came and closed the pub. There was no trouble at all, just exuberance. After that I just went on to the next pub. I regret not going up into town for the big celebrations. I remember feeling exhausted by the end of the final because of the strain of it all.

I am now living in Canada and have my ticket from the 1966 final set in an acrylic baseball card holder for display. It is a great conversation piece and people ask whether it is real. I reckon a fair number of people

Bobby Charlton at the post-match celebration.

from the final is still one of the most valuable things I possess – not in terms of money but in emotional terms.

D. West

I was eleven just five days before the World Cup final in 1966. I lived in Wembley, very handy for the ground. My father and brothers did spare time jobs sweeping the terraces for which they were rewarded with tickets for games. I was able to make use of one or two of these for earlier games and I was also able to go to the final itself. I am in quite a number of photographs as the youngster with a blue top on (Chelsea fan) and white rosette next to his dad right at the front of the little balcony over the players' tunnel. We were next to a German photographer, which upset my dad because he was never able to warm to the Germans after the war. After the game I remember proudly being patted on the head by Alf Ramsay as he went past on his way to an interview.

On the day after the final all the sweepers and helpers of various sorts went in to do their bit and then, when they had finished they had a mass game of about twenty-a-side on the very pitch where a matter of hours earlier England had won the World Cup. I was deemed too young to join in but when that game was all over I got a knockabout in one of the goalmouths. My two older brothers both played in the 'big' game.

J. Banks

have convinced themselves that they were there or pretend they were there when they were not. I have seen top level sport of various sorts all over the world but that World Cup final remains the high point of it all, followed by QPR appearing at Wembley the following year.

The week after the final I went to Germany to stay with friends. The place was awash with papers and magazines putting a German slant on it all and especially on the – as they saw it unfair – third goal.

I was at the final on my own because of the way and time I got the ticket, but then and celebrating afterwards with total strangers were still wildly happy. My ticket

I was only twelve in 1966. I was taken to the final and allowed in on my own. I was at the end by the tunnel and I remember there being great numbers of German fans there. Everyone was very friendly with lots of singing and banner waving and passing round of beer. You wouldn't get any of that nowadays what with segregation and a ban on alcohol. They wouldn't give me any because I was too young.

The family friend who came expecting to pick me up at the end of the game was able to walk straight into the ground in time to see the German equaliser and the whole of extra time and beyond, all without any ticket.

I. Short

I lived in Wembley in 1966 just a few streets away from the ground. All the years I was growing up, I remember hearing the roar from big games at the stadium. I was bought a ten-match ticket for the London games as a nineteenth birthday present by my mother. I still have all the tickets.

In the run-up to the final I developed a bronchial infection and my mother said I would be mad to go but nothing on earth would have stopped me. I was very excited by the chants of all the foreign fans and just seeing them there in numbers, especially the French. My hometown had become cosmopolitan.

My most vivid memory was of Bobby Moore actually lifting up the cup and the explosion of euphoria that followed. I also recall Nobby Stiles' little dance – it was all in such contrast to the feeling of despair when the Germans got their equaliser. On the evening of the final I went out with a girl called Gloria; I think that was her name. Ten days later I went to Germany and felt like a Pariah!

G. Lucas

I had a season ticket for all the Wembley games in 1966 and it cost me about £30. What price would even one game be nowadays? The main memory was of

Happy players' wives celebrate victory.

course Saturday July 30th when, after the victory, a group of us went from Wembley by tube to the Royal Garden Hotel where a great many other folk had gathered too. I think we all waited two or three hours, maybe longer, until at long last the team came out onto the balcony to receive an ovation the like of which I have never heard before or since. It brought a lump to my throat and I felt very proud to be English.

When they left we all made our way home to different places; we did not go into a pub like they do these days (celebrating these days is very different). I believe I saw the replay on the television later that evening.

Not a great number of folk are aware that it was my decision to have a programme printed specially for the World Cup final. The Football Association at that time did not have too much to do with programmes and the printers asked me after the semi-final against Portugal, whether or not we should have programmes printed for the final itself. You can guess what my reaction was. It was a sell out and a further reprint of 10,000 copies was done. At the time I was a programme dealer hence the decision to have the programmes printed on both occasions.

D. Stacey

I was fifteen at the time and I was a member of a local youth club, St Thomas More. The club had got four tickets for each game and everyone's name went into a draw to see who would get which tickets. I don't remember any cost being involved. I got the

The headline says it all.

opening game and the White City game and the final. Three other youngsters who drew tickets for the final sold theirs – one got £5 – and they urged me to do likewise, but of course I wouldn't.

I was behind the tunnel next to two lads from Newcastle. They were very friendly towards me. Two minutes before the end of normal time and confident that England had won they had to leave in order to catch a train. They missed the equaliser and all the drama of extra time.

D. Dwyer

I had obtained a ten-match ticket for the London group and went to all but one of the games. I missed the one at the White City. I was behind the goal where Hurst put his last goal in and would have caught the ball if it had kept going. I still have my tickets, programmes and souvenirs from that summer. Bobby Moore was absolutely brilliant, I thought.

In the tented village area outside Wembley I bumped into someone and when I looked to see who it was it turned out to be Ferenc Puskas. I have a clear recollection of Ratin being dismissed and of seeing Ramsay stopping the England players from exchanging shirts. I remember pummelling the man in front of me when we scored and he turned out to be a German. In my view the German equaliser came from a free kick that should never have been given, and in any case there was a handball before it was put into the net. England hadn't looked much in the early games. Ramsay's policy of keeping possession and playing it square gradually worked.

After the final no one wanted to go home. We eventually drove back to Somerset, from where we had driven up for each game. We met up with several other local footballers from the Wells area in a chip shop and then on to a pub to celebrate. Everywhere had a wonderful atmosphere.

E. Loxton

I bought a ten-match ticket but with living in Blyth I found it impossible to get to the games at Middlesbrough. It would have been fine if they had played at Newcastle as they had originally intended. I let someone else have the Ayresome Park games but went to all the games at Sunderland.

I then took a holiday in London for the last three games. I watched the West Germany game on the television on the Monday night then went to the wonderful semi-final at Wembley against Portugal, the play-off game and, of course, the final itself.

Only twice in my life have I completely lost my voice by the end of a game. The first was this World Cup final in 1966 when I just shouted myself hoarse. The other was at the time of Blyth Spartans' historic victory in their FA Cup tie at Stoke. At the final I found by remarkable coincidence that I was stood next to a friend also from Blyth. We travelled together after the game back into the centre of London and I often wonder if he thought it strange that I didn't seem to have much to say for myself on that journey. It was just that I had completely lost my voice and couldn't talk properly. They were happy

ALF THE GREATEST

3 years ago he tipped England to win the Cup. Yesterday they did

A headline acknowledging the nation's debt to Ramsay.

days. I still have all my tickets and other ephemera.

R. Clark

I went down on the train with my dad for the World Cup final. Before the game I went with him to the Wembley Conservative Club and remember Jimmy Hill and Johnny Haynes being in there and also that there was very heavy betting on England to win.

My dad got so worked up by the end of full time that he was standing on his seat yelling at the referee to blow for full time. We had good seats near the Royal Box and after the game we went out through the same gate as the players' wives. I remember quite a few of them trying to buy rosettes and the like from the fans because they hadn't had any opportunity to do so before the game.

P. Wilkinson

My husband and I were at nearly all the games of the 1966 World Cup and the memory of the final will live with me until I die; all of us shouting ourselves silly and what a lovely atmosphere. We took my nephew with us and he was only a teenager then.

At the time of the World Cup coming to England we had just sunk all our savings into buying a bungalow and were practically broke. We had a few pounds in the bank – just enough to get to the games. We tossed up and my husband said that we may never see another World Cup in England so we decided to go. Sadly, the World Cup final was to be the last game my husband saw World Cup wise as he died in 1972.

I will never forget the patriotism at Wembley and the sheer joy on the faces of the players. I still have my programme to treasure and I am still a season ticket holder with the best club in the world, Queens Park Rangers.

Mrs L. Dane

I was involved with the training programme at Lilleshall then joined up with everybody for the final. Alf invited me down. I looked after the ladies on the Friday and we all went to see a show starring Charlie Drake – *Charlie's Aunt* or some such. It was a bloody awful show anyway!

On the Saturday morning I went out to the Hendon Hall Hotel for lunch. As we were coming into London for the game I remember all the banners and all the fans cheering when they realised who was on the bus. The best banner that I remember was the one which said 'Nobby for Prime Minister'.

I was in the dressing room before and after the game and during the game I looked after the ladies. After the game I went on the bus to the banquet and all the way there sirens and car horns were sounding. This was a new experience in England.

All the wives and girlfriends were invited down just for the final. Alf got the FA to organise it so they could at least be there for that. The wives could not get into the banquet after the final as there simply wasn't room with four teams to fit in. I got in and ended up sitting next to Alf. Alf was a gentleman and very loyal and supportive to those who worked for him. He was, however, a hard taskmaster, determined to get his own way. He was an exceptional man, which was what was needed.

This was the highest thing that ever happened in English football. Looking back now there is a bit of a mist over it all, a bit like when you get married.

W. McGuiness

At the final I remember the noise being deafening; more so than at any other game. This does not really come across on the television. There was a chant that was sung at the final but again it does not really come across on the television – 'Ee-aye-addio, we won the war' and also, 'When the Reds come marching in'. Very, very occasionally the German supporters could be heard over to my right. I literally could not hear my own shouting. The following day my voice was lost. I was immediately adjacent to the players' tunnel, standing of course. Traditionally, as you know, most noise emanates from behind the goals.

I was never in doubt that we were going to win although Hurst's goal at the end came as a relief. His 'controversial' goal was clearly a goal as far as we were concerned as Hunt's reaction dictated that. If he, a very honest player, had been in any doubt, he would have put it in himself to make sure. The celebrations were delightful; who could forget Nobby and his jig. Afterwards, as I was leaving the area of the stadium the England coach went past very slowly and I got a good look at all the happy players

RIGHT ON TOP OF THE WORLD

England....4 West Germany....2

Page 32 SUNDAY MAIL, July 31, 1966

England were World Champions for the first (and so far only) time.

smiling and waving – magic.

Being a lifelong amateur photographer, I took my camera to the game and, of the photographs I took, by far the most interesting was one of Hurst's second, controversial goal. It seemed to me that a goal was highly likely so as the ball 'entered' the net I pressed the shutter. The ball has gone over the 'keeper's hands and is either about to hit the bar or is on the way down after having hit the bar. An expert could probably tell. Note the cigar in the hand of the spectator in front of me.

D.C. Jones

I was resigned to watching the final on the television when I got another letter from Wembley saying they had had some tickets returned, no doubt from departing fans of Brazil, and my name had been selected from the ballot. So I went to the final and stood on the lower terrace just by the tunnel to the right as you look at it. These were the days before supporters were segregated so we were all mixed up with the Germans. I remember I was standing next to two drunken Liverpool fans – they kept chanting Roger Hunt's name – who gave the nazi salute during the German national anthem. It seemed amusing at the time, now I would be embarrassed.

I always remember that while the teams were warming up before the kick off I was standing in acres of space, which I thought was strange. As the referee blew his whistle it seemed like hundreds of programme sellers, hot dog men, turnstile attendants came rushing in and suddenly it was packed. The atmosphere was fantastic. I remember England's first goal quite clearly as I was watching Hurst as Moore took the free kick. Nobody had picked him up and it looked as if it was something they'd done a hundred times on the West Ham training ground.

I also clearly remember the German equaliser. You never see it on the film of the match, except for the England defenders appealing to the referee, but the blond German left-back clearly handled the ball before it fell to Weber who scored.

Extra time was brilliant. If there was one player that won that match for England during those thirty minutes it was Alan Ball. You'd have thought he'd only just come on. He was everywhere: tackling, passing, shooting. Hurst may have got the goals but Ball was my man of the match and that was long before he became Pompey's manager!

I can't remember whether the third goal was or wasn't over the line. I was right behind it so I couldn't see. I suppose we all went along with Roger Hunt's reaction. Waiting for the Soviet linesman to make his decision was a very tense time, and it still is when you see the replay of it. The final goal was something else. Unlike Kenneth Wolstenholme I wasn't even aware that 'some people were on the pitch'. We were all focused on Geoff Hurst's run.

Obviously I stayed on for the presentation and celebrations and as I was right next to the tunnel I saw them all go in. It was certainly a game I will never forget. I have the video in black and white.

This leads me to a story that a friend told me. His father was an outside broadcast cameraman. Although colour televisions were rare in those days, the BBC did have a colour outside broadcast unit but it had already been booked to cover a flower show or something that day. The only units available were for black and white.

S. Saul

At the pre-banquet gathering at the Royal Garden Hotel, the Portuguese star Eusebio was in the basement corridor with a wad of personal action photographs in hand, signing each and distributing to fans – I have one of them. Many of the 400 plus throng were asking the non-English speaking Russian linesman, Bakhramov, whether it was over the line – as if he could ever be persuaded to say 'Niet' at that stage! At the late stages of the banquet, George Brown – by then a notorious wino and West Ham fan – was dancing on his table singing 'I'm forever blowing bubbles'. Hugh McIlvanney later wrote 'With Harold Wilson about to follow up his credit squeeze by appointing George Brown Foreign Secretary, there seemed a chance that Alf Ramsay would take over the country De Gaulle style'.

W. Goss, AFA.

I could hardly believe the way it had all worked out. I had put in my application for a ten-match ticket the very minute it became possible to do so. Whoever ended up in the final I was determined to be there. In the event, of course, it was England with the whole nation galvanised by their success and progress towards the fulfilment of

Some of those who didn't go to celebrate in the streets went to shows such as this one.

Ramsay's promise.

I had gone down to London for the last three games, so by the end of the week, on World Cup final day, I considered myself entirely *au fait* with travel to the ground and so forth. There had been no problems going to the semi and play-off games, though in both cases my friend, a calming influence, had gone with me (and ended up getting last minute tickets for the games). There was no way he would get a ticket for the final so I went on my own having arranged to meet him in town afterwards. Such was my nervous state that I got on the wrong train. Such was my obsession about not ever being late that I had plenty of time to sort that out and get to the stadium before the gates opened.

Inside I was amazed to find myself next to another friend whom I had not noticed there at the two previous games that week. He was the devoted secretary of the supporters club of my beloved hometown team of Blyth Spartans. We shared all the emotional ups and downs of that remarkable afternoon when time at one moment seemed to be standing still, yet at another racing by. Much of the detail is something of a blur coloured by countless video replays. The deflation when Germany equalised was almost too much to bear; the tension waiting for the verdict on the third goal was endless and then the final all-embracing euphoria when Hurst crashed the fourth and unequivocally winning goal home just in front of us.

Bobby Moore looked a small distant figure as he was given the trophy by the Queen, whom I had never previously seen live, but even through the tears my vision of the unique moment when the trophy was raised aloft was and remains crystal clear. We travelled back to the centre of London together; my friend strangely quiet (because he had shouted himself hoarse as I later discovered).

We had already decided to go for a meal and a show. It simply never occurred to me that we could try to see the team and the trophy, nor to go to the crowded centres of celebration such as Trafalgar Square. *The Black and White Minstrel Show* at the Victoria Palace was chosen, as much as anything because one of the minstrels came from Blyth. I remember we had seats very high up in the theatre and enjoyed the show. I toasted England with a large brandy I seem to recall and we made our way back to our hostel in Kentish Town some time after midnight on an all night bus.

I have subsequently seen games at Wembley in all sorts of circumstances – VIP box, sponsor's guest and so on but nothing could ever really match the pure magic of 1966.

N. Shiel

CHAPTER 4

Aftermath

This section includes only a very few individual memories but is rather a brief pictorial panorama of just some of the ways in which England's triumph of 1966 had had a subsequent impact. The national team has since then always been somewhat in the shadow of Ramsay's heroes and, presumably, will carry on being so until such time as another England captain lifts the World Cup. Geoff Hurst and especially Bobby Charlton worked tirelessly to promote England's bid for the 2006 finals to be played here, although sadly to no avail

Interest in all aspects of football memorabilia has continued to grow and, in recent years, grow dramatically. This, together with the nostalgia born of the passage of time and the intensification of focus caused by the 2006 campaign, has meant that all 1966 memorabilia has now become very much sought after. From the humblest World Cup Willie beer mat up to star items such as a winners' shirt, cap, or even medal, prices have soared. Sadly, if inevitably, some of this is connected with the passing on of those concerned. Memorabilia from the England trainer Harold Shepherdson made some very high prices when it came up for auction with even obscure items such as kit bags being eagerly fought over by collectors. The star item there was the pennant which Bobby Moore received from his German opposite number before the final itself, and which Moore later gave to Shepherdson. Moore's own memorabilia has been the subject of a somewhat squalid dispute since his untimely death; still not resolved as this book goes to press.

On a much more humble level most of the contributors to this book still have the sort of things which were, are and probably always will be treasured souvenirs. They have their tickets, programmes, bits and pieces of merchandise, newspapers and scrap-books and so on. Now a whole generation of collectors is keen to obtain all these things and so prices rise. Of course those who were there can sell their souvenirs but that which is even more precious than those, albeit not in financial terms, is the memory of it all. When a collector buys a ticket or a shirt, depending on his means, he acquires a tangible link with a great event. When he listens to or reads about it from someone who was there, then he gets much closer.

The World Cup (1966) Association has quietly kept alive the true spirit of that great year and even as its numbers dwindle through the passing of time it, perhaps more than any other, remains the best window on the summer of '66 as a whole. If you have the money you can go on a cruise with a number of the players from 1966 and maybe they will be sufficiently freed from the constraints of their agents to give some frank reminiscences.

Watch the video, collect the memorabilia, look forward to the next time, but in order to

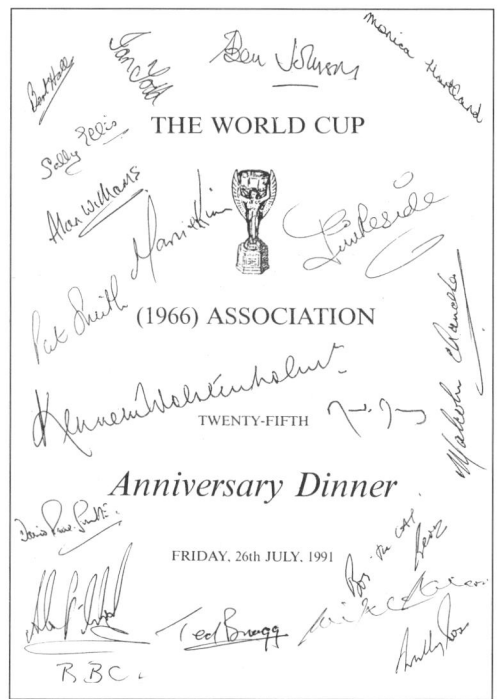

Left: *Signed menu card from a twenty-fifth anniversary dinner.* Right: *J. Heywood re-enacting 1966.*

understand what it was really all about read the memories and maybe go out and find some more.

I was a reporter on the *Sheffield Star* during the World Cup and was called out to do quite a number of stories, so I have a number of pleasant memories. One particular story brought me a rich reward I never could have imagined. At the start of the World Cup I met an eighteen year old German fan who had cycled from near his home, a small German town near Frankfurt. It was in the evening and he was looking for camping. He had only reached the Eastern end of the city and the only camping was many miles further on in the Peak district. I took him home to stay the night and he stayed with me for the rest of the World Cup. We have remained close friends for the rest of our lives and he is godfather to my daughter. At the Wembley final we walked to the stadium together with Union and German flags and stood together through all the emotions of the match. After nearly forty years we still regularly visit and telephone each other.

R. Redden

I was not at any of the games, but my father who died some years ago went to all the England games including the final and I have his ticket stub from that game with me. One of my last memories of him was sitting together and watching a black and white rerun of the final, with him pointing out where he stood and so on.

I. Prime

Thank you very much for lending me the old fashioned football. I was Geoff Hurst in our schools' Autumn Performance. Each class took a decade and acted out some news items about it. We did the 1960s. There was the war in Vietnam, flower power, the first walk on the moon and the 1966 World Cup.

J. Heywood, writing in 1995

I was an England supporter and member of the supporters club in 1966. I have been a Villa supporter since 1928. I saw all England's games and with me at the final were my son and daughter. I was invited to one of the dinners they held and I have a photograph of me holding the World Cup. I have many souvenirs of World Cup 1966.

M. Jackson

Fans with the trophy at an England Supporters' dinner.

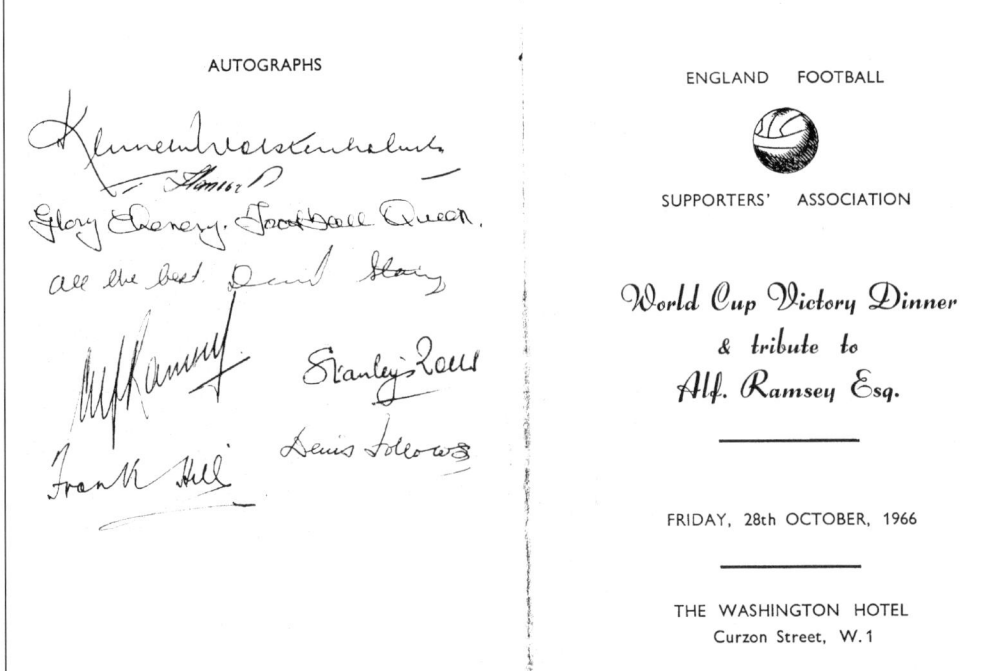

A menu from the England Supporters' Club dinner, signed by Woolstenholme, Ramsay, Rous and others.

Menu

🞼

Hors d'ôeuvres variés

Coquille St. Jacques

Dindonneau roti à l'anglaise
Pomme duchesse
Choux de bruxelles

Apple strudel
Ice Cream

Café

Toasts

THE QUEEN

Proposed by   P. Hancock, Esq.
                                 The Treasurer.

🞼

ALF. RAMSEY, ESQ.

Proposed by   Tony Pullein, Esq.
                                 The President.

Response by   Alf. Ramsey, Esq.

🞼

THE ENGLAND FOOTBALL SUPPORTERS' ASSOCIATION

Proposed by   Sir Stanley Rous, C.B.E.
                                 President of F.I.F.A.

Response by   The Treasurer

🞼

OUR GUESTS

Proposed by   Kenneth Wolstenholme, Esq.
                                 B.B.C.

Response by   Cyril Jackson, Esq.
                                 "The Football Referee"

England Supporters' Club menu.

A collection of memorabilia from 1966.

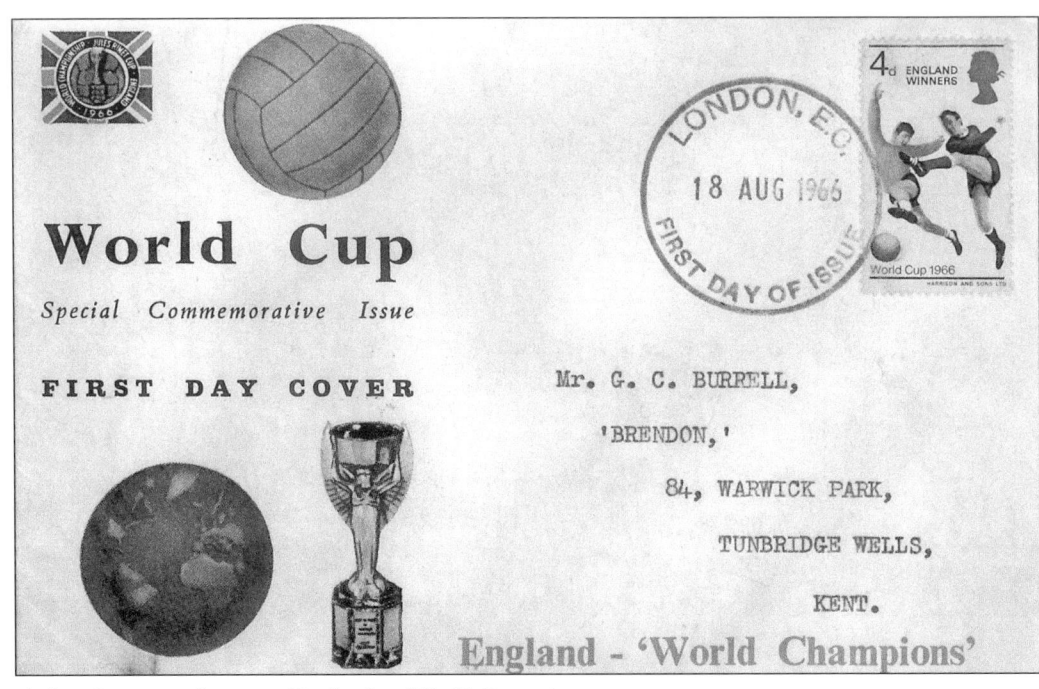

A first day cover featuring England as World Cup winners.

A postcard issued by the Post Office to promote their Millennium stamps.

Eusebio is presented with his award by Harold Wilson.

I found that even shortly afterwards people were not inclined to believe that I had been to the World Cup final. At University only a couple of years after the final people were all too ready to assume I was making it up for effect. Over the (now many) years since attitudes have mellowed, few disbelieve and, especially, one's pupils at school are in some awe. To them it seems both familiar from the footage yet very remote in time, a bit like the war. I remember interviewing Dick Pym, last surviving player from the 1923 first Wembley Cup final and certainly there was a similar awe; in his case of course deserved as he was a great player not just a humble fan. Even so there is a certain inherent determination to become very old just so one can feel increasingly special when saying, fifty, sixty, even seventy years on, 'I was there!' At the last Wembley Cup final I found myself with an all areas pass, interviewed by ITV on the balcony beneath the twin towers, bumping into Sir Geoff Hurst in the banqueting hall and able to go down through the Queen's lounge round the pitch to the players' tunnel. Much of that became possible on the Wembley tours, but to do it all in the context of a big match made me think back to 1966 when I was a distant speck among a great many others behind one of the goals and others, many of whose memories are preserved in this book, were in the 'front line'.

As for the players, it was very special to see not one but two World Cup stars in Nobby and Bobby playing in the FA Cup at Blyth when they were with Preston. Much later, Bally became manager at Exeter and I got to know him a little and even set up a training session for the City players at Exeter School on our all weather pitch prior to a visit to Deepdale, which in those days was an artificial surface. It worked as Exeter won comfortably and I got my photograph taken with a World Cup hero.

All in all I feel very, very fortunate to have been at those 1966 games and most especially the final. Whatever happens, nothing can ever take that away.

N. Shiel

Programme cover for the game held after the terrible fire at Bradford.

Alan Ball as manager of Exeter City.

A postcard given out by Geoff Hurst to promote one of his business interests and showing him with a selection of memorabilia.

Alan Ball with the author at Exeter School during a Grecians training session.

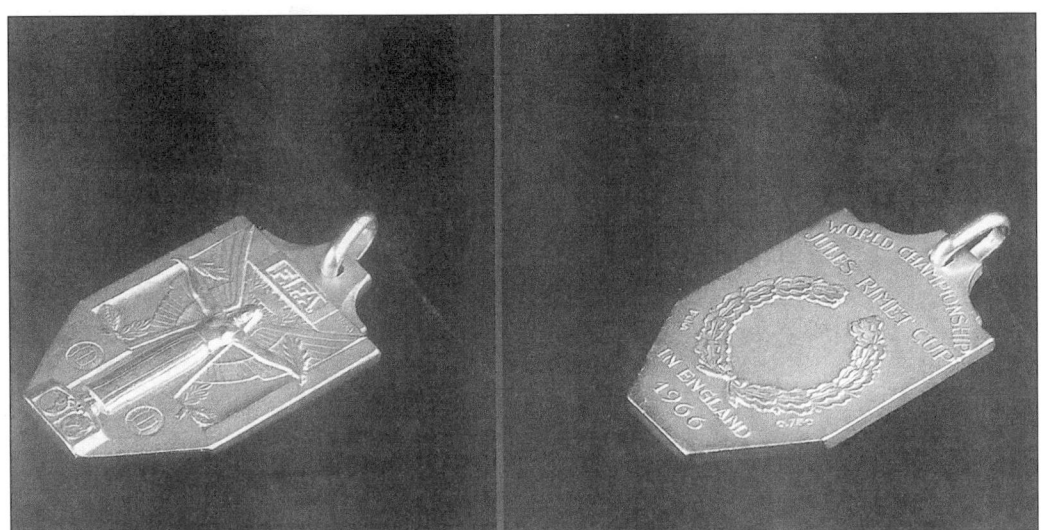

A winners' medal from 1966.

An England cap from the 1966 World Cup campaign.

An England and West German shirt from the 1966 World Cup final.

The cover of an auction catalogue of memorabilia which included many items from the 1966 England trainer, Harold Shepherdson, such as the pennant exchanged before the final itself.

Kenneth Wolstenholme, now semi-retired, at his Devon home.

The logo for the sadly unsuccessful campaign to bring the World Cup back to England.

Appendix 1

Accommodation and training quarters of final series teams

	Accommodation	Training Quarters

Group One

England	Hendon Hall Hotel Ashley Lane London NW4	Arsenal FC Wembley FC Bank of England sports ground Roehampton
France	Homestead Court Hotel Homestead Lane Welwyn Garden City Hertfordshire	Gosling Stadium Welwyn Garden City BAC Sports Centre Knebworth
Mexico	Alexandra National Hotel 330 Seven Sisters Road, London N4	Finchley FC Tottenham Hotspur FC
Uruguay	Saxon Inn Hotel Harlow, Essex	Harlow Sports Centre

Group Two

Argentine	Albany Hotel Birmingham	Police Training Centre Birmingham
W. Germany	Peveril of the Peak Hotel Dovedale Thorpe, near Ashbourne Derbyshire	Ashbourne FC Derby County FC
Spain	Penns Hall Hotel Penns Lane Walmley Sutton Coldfield Warwickshire	Delta Metal Co. Holly Lane Erdington Birmingham

Switzerland	Hallam Tower Hotel Fulwood Road Sheffield	Sheffield FC Sheffield University

Group Three

Brazil	Lymm Hotel Lymm Cheshire	Bolton Wanderers FC Lymm Grammar School
Bulgaria	Mollington Banastre Hotel Parkgate Road Chester	Chester FC
Hungary	Palace Hotel Birkdale Southport	Southport FC
Portugal	Stanneylands Hotel Wilmslow Cheshire	Stockport County FC

Group Four

Chile	Five Bridges Hotel High Street West Gateshead	Gateshead FC
Italy	School of Agriculture Hougall Durham	Hougall Agricultural College
N. Korea	The St George Hotel Tees-side Airport Near Darlington	ICI Sports Ground, Billingham
USSR	Grey College Durham	Durham University

Appendix 2
Results and Details

Group One

Match 1: Wembley Stadium, Monday 11 July

England 0   Uruguay 0

ENGLAND   URUGUAY

Gordon Banks   Ladislao Mazurkieviez
George Cohen   Horatio Troche
John Charlton   Luis Ubinas
Robert Moore   Jorge Manicera
Ramon Wilson   Nestor Goncalvez
Norbert Stiles   Omar Caetano
Robert Charlton   Milton Viera
Alan Ball   Julio Cortes
James Greaves   Pedro Rocha
Roger Hunt   Hector Silva
John Connelly   Domingo Perez

Referee: Istvan Zsolt (Hungary)
Linesmen: Dimiter Roumentchev (Bulgaria), Tofik Bakhramov (USSR)
Attendance: 87,148 (receipts £67,974 12s 6d)

Match 5: Wembley Stadium, Wednesday 13 July

France (0)1   Mexico (0)1
Hausser   Borja

FRANCE

Marcel Aubour
Jean Djorkaeff
Robert Budzinski
Marcel Artelasa
Gabriel de Michele
Bernard Bosquier
Robert Herbin
Joseph Bonnel
Nestor Combin
Philippe Gondet
Gerard Hausser

MEXICO

Ignacio Calderon
Arturo Chaires
Gustavo Pena
Gabriel Nunez
Guillermo Hernandez
Isidoro Diaz
Magdaleno Mercado
Salvador Reyes
Enrique Borja
Javier Fragoso
Aaron Padilla

Referee: Menachem Ashkenasi (Israel)
Linesmen: Dr Karol Galba (Czechoslovakia), Joaquim Fernandez Campos (Portugal)

Attendance: 69,237 (£54,856 13s 0d)

Match 9: White City Stadium, Friday 15 July

Uruguay (2)2   France (1)1
Rocha, Cortes De Bourgoing (pen.)

URUGUAY

Ladislao Mazurkieviez
Horacio Troche
Luis Ubinas
Nestor Goncalvez
Jorge Manicera
Omar Milton
Viera Caetano
Julio Cortes
Pedro Rocha
Jose Sacia
Hector Domingo Perez

FRANCE

Marcel Aubour
Jean Djorkaeff
Marcel Artelasa
Robert Budzinski
Bernard Bosquier
Joseph Bonnel
Jaques Simon
Yves Herbert
Phillipe Gondet
De Bourgoing,
Gerard Hausser

Referee: Dr Karol Galba (Czechoslovakia)
Linesmen: Armando Marques (Brazil), Leo Callaghan (Wales)
Attendance: 45,662 (£31,667 16s 6d)

Match 13: Wembley Stadium, Saturday 16 July

Mexico (0)0   England (1)2
                Charlton, R., Hunt

MEXICO   ENGLAND

Ignacio Calderon   Gordon Banks
Jesus Del Muro   George Cohen
Guillermo Hernandez   John Charlton
Gustavo Pena   Robert Moore
Gabriel Nunez   Ramon Wilson
Arturo Chaires   Norbert Stiles
Isidoro Diaz   Robert Charlton
Ignacio Jauregui   Terence Paine
Salvador Reyes   James Greaves
Enrique Borja   Roger Hunt
Aaron Padilla   Martin Peters

Referee: Concetto Lo Bello (Italy)
Linesmen: Menachem Ashkenasi (Israel), Choi Duk Ryong (North Korea)
Attendance: 92,570 (£71,105 14s 0d)

Match 17: Wembley Stadium, Tuesday 19 July.

Mexico 0 Uruguay 0

MEXICO

Antonio Carvajal
Arturo Chaires
Gustavo Pena
Gabriel Nunez
Guillermo Hernandez
Isidoro Diaz
Magdalenp Mercado
Salvador Reyes
Ernesto Cisneros
Enrique Borja
Aaron Padilla

URUGUAY

Ladislao Mazurkieviez
Horatio Troche
Jorge Manicera
Luis Ubinas
Nextor Goncalvez
Omar Caetano
Julio Cortes
Milton Viera
Jose Sacia
Pedro Rocha
Domingo Perez

Referee: Bertil Loow (Sweden)
Linesmen: Concetto Lo Bello (Italy), Claudo Vicuna (Chile)
Attendance: 61,112 (£47,375 0s 6d)

Match 21: Wembley Stadium, Wednesday 20 July.

France (0)0   England (1)2
              (Hunt 2)

FRANCE

Marcel Aubour
Jean Djorkaeff
Marcel Artelasa
Robert Budzinski
Joseph Bonnel
Bernard Bosquier
Robert Herbin
Jacques Simon
Yves Herbet
Philippe Gondet
Gerard Hausser

ENGLAND

Gordon Banks
George Cohen
John Charlton
Robert Moore
Ramon Wilson
Norbert Stiles
Robert Charlton
Ian Callaghan
James Greaves
Roger Hunt
Martin Peters

Referee: Arturo Yamasaki (Peru)
Linesmen: Dr. Karol Galba (Czechoslovakia), Dimiter Roumentchev (Bulgaria)
Attendance: 98,270 (£77,328 3s 0d)

GROUP ONE - FINAL POSITIONS

	P	W	D	L	F	A	Pts
England	3	2	1	0	4	0	5
Uruguay	3	1	2	0	2	1	4
Mexico	3	0	2	1	1	3	2
France	3	0	1	2	2	5	1

Group Two

Match 2: Hillsborough, Tuesday 12 July

West Germany (3)   5 Switzerland (0)0
  Held
  Haller 2 (1 pen.)
  Beckenbauer 2

WEST GERMANY   SWITZERLAND

Hans Tilkowski   Charles Elsener
Horst Hottges   Andre Grobety
Karl-Heinz Schellinger   Heinz Schneiter
Franz Beckenbauer   Ely Tacchella
Willi Schulz   Hansruedi Fuhrer
Wolfgang Weber   Heinz Bani
Albert Brulls   Richard Durr
Helmut Haller   Karl Odermatt
Uwe Seeler   Robert Hosp
Wolfgang Overath   Fritz Kunzli
Siegried Held   Jean-Claude Schindelholz

Referee: Hugh Philips (Scotland)
Linesmen: John Adair (Northern Ireland), Bertil Loow (Sweden)
Attendance: 36,127 (£28,515 1s 6d)

Match 6: Villa Park, Wednesday 13 July

Spain (0)1   Argentine (0)2
 Martinez   Artime (2)

SPAIN   ARGENTINE

Jose Iribar   Antonio Roma
Manuel Sanchis   Roberto Perfumo
Eladio Silvestre   Silvio Marzolini
Jose Martinez   Roberto Ferreiro
Francisco Fernandez   Antonio Ratin
Ignacio Zoco   Jorge Albrecht
Jose Ufarte   Jorge Solari
Luis Del Sol   Alberto Gonzalez
Joaquin Peiro   Luis Artime
Luis Suarez   Ermindo Onega
Francisco Gento   Oscar Mas

Referee: Dimiter Roumentchev (Bulgaria)
Linesmen: Arturo Yamasaki (Peru), Konstantin Zecevic (Yugoslavia)
Attendance: 47,982 (£36,254 1s 0d)

Match 10: Hillsborough, Friday 15 July

Switzerland (1)   1 Spain (0)2
 Quentin   Sanchis, Amaro

SWITZERLAND   SPAIN

Charles Elsener   Jose Iribar
Rene Brodmann   Manuel Sanchis
Hansruedi Fuhrer   Ignacio Zoco
Werner Leimgruber   Jose Martinez
Kurt Armbruster   Severino Reija
Xaver Stierli   Francisco Fernandez
Heinz Bani   Luis Suarez
Jakob Kuhn   Luis Del Sol
Vittore Gottardi   Amancio Amaro
Robert Hosp   Joaquin Peiro
Rene-Pierre Quentin   Francisco Gento

Referee: Tofik Bakhramov (USSR)
Linesmen: Istvan Zsolt (Hungary), Hugh Philips (Scotland)
Attendance: 32,028 (£25,528 6s 0d)

Match 14: Villa Park, Saturday 16 July

Argentine 0 West Germany 0

ARGENTINE	WEST GERMANY
Antonio Roma	Hans Tilkowski
Roberto Perfumo	Horst Hottges
Silvio Marzolini	Willi Schulz
Roberto Ferreiro	Wolfgang Weber
Jorge Albrecht	Karl-Heinz Schnellinger
Antonio Ratin	Helmut Haller
Alberto Gonzalez	Franz Beckenbauer
Jorge Solari	Albert Brulls
Luis Artime	Uwe Seeler
Ermindo Onega	Wolfgang Overath
Oscar Mas	Siegfried Held

Referee: Konstantin Zecevic (Yugoslavia)
Linesmen: Joaquim Fernandes Campos (Portugal), Bertil Loow (Sweden)
Attendance: 51,419 (£38,164 6s 6d)

Match 18: Hillsborough, Tuesday 19 July

Argentine (0)2 Switzerland (0)0
Artime, Onega

ARGENTINE	SWITZERLAND
Antonio Roma	Leo Eichmann
Roberto Perfumo	Hansruedi Fuhrer
Roberto Ferreiro	Rene Brodmann
Oscar Calics	Kurt Armbruster
Silvio Marzolini	Xaver Stierli
Alberto Gonzalez	Heinz Bani
Antonio Ratin	Jakob Kuhn
Jorge Solari	Vittore Gottardi
Ermindo Onega	Robert Hosp
Luis Artime	Fritz Kunzli
Oscar Mas	Rene-Pierre Quentin

Referee: Joaquim Fernandes Campos (Portugal)
Linesmen: Tofik Bakhramov (USSR), Istvan Zsolt (Hungary)
Attendance: 31,443 (£24,649 16s 0d)

Match 22: Villa Park, Wednesday 20 July

Spain (1)1   West Germany (1)2
Fuste   Emmerich, Seeler

SPAIN	WEST GERMANY
Jose Iribar	Hans Tilkowski
Manuel Sanchis	Horst Hottges
Severino Reija	Willi Schulz
Jesus Glaria	Wolfgang Weber
Francisco Fernandez	Karl-Heinz Schnellinger
Ignacio Zoco	Franz Beckenbauer
Adelardo Rodriguez	Wolfgang Overath
Jose Fuste	Werner Kramer
Amancio Amaro	Uwe Seeler
Marcelino Martinez	Siegfried Held
Carlos Lapetra	Lothar Emmerich

Referee: Armando Marques (Brazil)
Linesmen: Claudio Vicuna (Chile), Choi Duk Ryong (North Korea)
Attendance: 51,875 (£38,414 7s 6d)

GROUP TWO - FINAL POSITIONS

	P	W	D	L	F	A	Pts
W. Germany	3	2	1	0	7	1	5
Argentine	3	2	1	0	4	1	5
Spain	3	1	0	2	4	5	2
Switzerland	3	0	0	3	1	9	0

Group Three

Match 3: Goodison Park, Tuesday 12 July

Bulgaria (0)   0   Brazil (1) 2
                    Pele, Garrincha

BULGARIA

George Naidenov
Alexander Shalamanov
Ivan Vutzov
Dimiter Penev
Boris Gaganelov
Stoyan Kitov
Peter Zhekov
Dinko Dermendjiev
George Asparuhov
Dimiter Yakimov
Ivan Kolev

BRAZIL

Gylmar
Djalma Santos
Bellini
Altair
Paulo Henrique
Denilson
Lima
Garrincha
Alcindo
Pele
Jairzinho

Referee: Kurt Tschenscher (West Germany)
Linesmen: George McCabe (England), John Taylor (England)
Attendance: 52,847 (£40,552 15s 6d)

Match 7: Old Trafford, Wednesday 13 July

Hungary (0)1   Portugal (1)3
Bene   Augusto 2, Torres

HUNGARY

Antal Szentmihalyi
Sandor Matrai
Beno Kaposzta
Kalman Sovari
Kalman Meszoly
Ferenc Sipos
Ferenc Bene
Antal Nagy
Florian Albert
Janos Farkas
Gyula Rakosi

PORTUGAL

Joaquim Carvalho
Joao Morais
Alexandre Baptista
Vicente Lucas
Hilario Conceicao
Jaime Graca
Mario Coluna
Jose Augusto
Eusebio Ferreira
Jose Torres
Antonio Simoes

Referee: Leo Callaghan (Wales)
Linesmen: William Clements (England), Kevin Howley (England)
Attendance: 37,311 (£30,407 2s 0d)

Match 11: Goodison Park, Friday 15 July

BRAZIL (1)1   Hungary (1)3
Tostao   Bene, Farkas, Meszoly (pen.)

BRAZIL

Gylmar
Djalma Santos
Bellini
Altair
Paulo Henrique
Gerson
Lima
Garrincha
Alcindo
Tostao
Jairzinho

HUNGARY

Joszef Gelei
Beno Kaposzta
Sandor Matrai
Kalman Meszoly
Gustav Szepesi-Szedunka
Imre Mathesz
Ferenc Sipos
Ferenc Bene
Florian Albert
Janos Farkas
Gyula Rakosi

Referee: Kenneth Dagnall (England)
Linesmen: Kevin Howley (England), Arturo Yamasaki (Peru)
Attendance: 57,455 (£46,053 3s 0d)

Match 15, Old Trafford, Saturday 16 July

Portugal 3(2)   Bulgaria (0)0
Vutzov (o.g.)
Eusebio
Torres)

PORTUGAL

BULGARIA

Jose Pereira
Alberto Festa
Germano Figueiredo
Vicente Lucas
Hilario Conceicao
Jaime Graca
Mario Coluna
Jose Augusto
Eusebio Ferreira
Jose Torres
Antonio Simoes

George Naidenov
Alexander Shalamanov
Dimiter Penev
Ivan Vutzov
Boris Gaganelov
Dobromir Zhechev
Dimiter Yakimov
Dinko Dermendjiev
Peter Zhekov
George Asparuhov
Alexander Kostov

Referee: Jose Maria Codesal (Uruguay)
Linesmen: Roberto Goicoechea (Argentine), Kurt Tschenscher (West Germany)
Attendance: 33,355 (£27,713 15s 0d)

Match 19, Goodison Park, Tuesday 19 July

Portugal (2)3   Brazil (0)1
Simoes, Eusebio 2   Rildo

PORTUGAL   BRAZIL

Jose Pereira   Manga
Joao Morais   Fidelis
Alexandre Baptista   Brito
Vicente Lucas   Orlando
Hilario Conceicao   Rildo
Jaime Graca   Denilson
Mario Coluna   Lima
Jose Augusto   Jairzinho
Eusebio Ferreira   Silva
Jose Torres   Pele
Antonio Simoes   Parana

Referee: George McCabe (England)
Linesmen: Leo Callaghan (Wales), Kenneth Dagnall (England)
Attendance: 62,204 (£49,635 13s 6d)

Match 23, Old Trafford, Wednesday 20 July

Hungary (2)3   Bulgaria (1)1
Davidov (o.g.)   (Asparuhov)
Meszoly, Bene

HUNGARY   BULGARIA

Jozsef Gelei   Simeon Simeonov
Beno Kaposzta   Dimiter Penev
Sandor Matrai   Dimiter Largov
Kalman Meszoly   Ivan Vutzov
Gustav Szepesi-Szedunka   Boris Gaganelov
Imre Mathesz   Dobromir Zhechev
Ferenc Sipos   Ivan Davidov
Ferenc Bene   Peter Zhekov
Florian Albert   George Asparuhov
Janos Farkas   Nikola Kotkov
Gyula Rakosi   Ivan Kolev

Referee: Roberto Goicoechea (Argentine)
Linesmen: Juan Gardeazabal (Spain), Jose Maria Codesal (Uruguay)
Attendance: 33,064 (£28,001 4s 6d)

GROUP THREE - FINAL POSITIONS

	P	W	D	L	F	A	Pts
Portugal	3	3	0	0	9	2	6
Hungary	3	2	0	1	7	5	4
Brazil	3	1	0	2	4	6	2
Bulgaria	3	0	0	3	1	8	0

Group Four

Match 4, Ayresome Park, Tuesday 12 July

USSR (2)3   North Korea (0)0
Malofeev 2
Banishevskiy

USSR	NORTH KOREA
Anzor Kavazashvili	Li Chan Myung
Vladimir Ponomarev	Pak Li Sup
Albert Shesternev	Shin Yung Kyoo
Murtaz Khurtsilava	Kang Bong Chil
Leonid Ostrovoskiy	Lim Loong Sun
Iosef Sabo	Im Seung Hwi
Georgiy Sichinava	Pak Seung Zin
Igor Chislenko	Han Bong Zin
Anatoliy Banishevskiy	Pak Doo Ik
Eduard Malofeev	Kang Ryong Woon
Galimzjan Khusainov	Kim Seung Il

Referee: Juan Gardeazabal (Spain)
Linesmen: Aly Kandil (UAR), Gottfried Dienst (Switzerland)
Attendance: 22,568 (£15,585 13s 6d)

Match 8, Roker Park, Wednesday 13 July

Chile (0)0   Italy (1)2
             Mazzola
             Barison

CHILE   ITALY

Juan Olivares   Enrico Albertosi
Luis Eyzaguirre   Tarcisio Burgnich
Humberto Cruz   Giacinto Facchetti
Elias Figueroa   Roberto Rosato
Hugo Villanueva   Sandro Salvadore
Ignacio Prieto   Giovanni Lodetti
Ruben Marcos   Marino Perani
Pedro Araya   Giacomo Bulgarelli
Armando Tobar   Sandro Mazzola
Albert Fouilloux   Giovanni Rivera
Leonel Sanchez   Paolo Barison

Referee: Gottfried Dienst (Switzerland)
Linesmen: Rudolf Kreitlein (West Germany), Jame Finney (England)
Attendance: 30,956 (£21,736 3s 0d)

Match 12, Ayresome Park, Friday 15 July

North Korea (0)1   Chile (1)1
Pak Seung Zin   Marcos (pen.)

NORTH KOREA   CHILE

Li Chan Myung   Juan Olivares
Pak Li Sup   Alberto Valentini
Shin Yung Kyoo   Humberto Kruz
Lim Zoong Sun   Elias Figueroa
Oh Yung Kwung   Hugo Villanueva
Pak Seung Zin   Ignacio Prieto
Im Seung Hwi   Ruben Marcos
Han Bong Zin   Alberto Fouilloux
Pak Doo Ik   Honorino Landa
Li Dong Woon   Pedro Araya
Kim Seung Il   Leonel Sanchez

Referee: Aly Kandil (UAR)
Linesmen: Ernest Crawford (England), James Finney (England)
Attendance: 15,887 (£11,664 3s 6d)

Match 16, Roker Park, Saturday 16 July

Italy (0)0   USSR (0)1
(Chislenko)

ITALY	USSR
Enrico Albertosi	Lev Yashin
Sandro Salvadore	Vladimir Ponomarev
Tarcisio Burgnich	Albert Shesternev
Roberto Rosata	Murtaz Khurtsilava
G. Franco Leoncini	Vasiliy Danilov
Giacinto Facchetti	Iosif Sabo
Giovanni Lodetti	Valeriy Voronin
Giacomo Bulgarelli	Igor Chislenko
Luigi Meroni	Eduard Malofeev
Sandro Mazzola	Anatoliy Banishevskiy
Ezio Pascutti	Galimzjan Khusainov

Referee: Rudolf Kreitlein (West Germany)
Linesmen: Aly Kandil (UAR), Ernest Crawford (England)
Attendance: 31,989 (£22,317 8s 0d)

Match 20, Ayresome Park, Tuesday 19 July

Italy (0)0   North Korea (1)1
Pak Doo Ik

ITALY   NORTH KOREA

Enrico Albertosi   Li Chan Myung
Spartaco Landini   Sim Zoong Sun
Francesco Janich   Shin Yung Kyoo
Aristide Guarneri   Ha Jung Won
Giacinto Facchetti   Oh Yoon Kwung
Giacomo Bulgarelli   Im Seung Hwi
Romano Fogli   Pak Seung Zin
Marino Perani   Han Bong Zin
Sandro Mazzola   Pak Doo Ik
Giovanni Rivera   Kim Bong Hwan
Paolo Barison   Yang Sung Kook

Referee: Pierre Schwinte (France)
Linesmen: John Adair (Northern Ireland), John Taylor (England)
Attendance: 18,727 (£13,096 15s 0d)

Match 24, Roker Park, Wednesday 20 July

Chile (1)1   USSR (1)2
Marcos   Porkujan 2

CHILE   USSR

Juan Olivares   Anzor Kavazashvili
Alberto Valentini   Victor Getmanov
Humberto Cruz   Alberto Shesternev
Elias Figueroa   Alexey Korneev
Hugo Villanueva   Leonid Ostrovskiy
Ruben Marcos   Valeriy Voronin
Ignacio Prieto   Valentin Afonin
Pedro Araya   Slava Metreveli
Honorino Landa   Victor Serebrjannikov
Guillermo Yavar   Eduard Markarov
Leonel Sanchez   Valeriy Porkujan

Referee: John Adair (Northern Ireland)
Linesmen: William Clements (England), Pierre Schwinte (France)
Attendance: 22,590 (£15,977 1s 0d)

GROUP FOUR - FINAL POSITIONS

	P	W	D	L	F	A	Pts
USSR	3	3	0	0	6	1	6
North Korea	3	1	1	1	2	4	3
Italy	3	1	0	2	2	2	2
Chile	3	0	1	2	2	5	1

Quarter-Finals

Match 25, Wembley Stadium, Saturday 23 July

England (0)1 Argentine (0)0
(Hurst)

ENGLAND	ARGENTINE
Gordon Banks	Antonio Roma
George Cohen	Roberto Ferreiro
John Charlton	Roberto Perfumo
Robert Moore	Jorge Albrecht
Ramon Wilson	Silvio Marzolini
Norbert Stiles	Alberto Gonzalez
Robert Charlton	Antonio Ratin
Alan Ball	Jorge Solari
Geoffrey Hurst	Luis Artime
Roger Hunt	Ermindo Onega
Martin Peters	Oscar Mas

Referee: Rudolf Kreitlein (West Germany)
Linesmen: Gottfried Dienst (Switzerland), Istvan Zsolt (Hungary).
Attendance: 90,584. Receipts: £97,561

Match 26, Hillsborough, Saturday 23 July

West Germany (1)4   Uruguay (0)0
Held, Beckenbauer Seeler, Haller

WEST GERMANY   URUGUAY

Hans Tilkowski   Ladislao Mazurkieviez
Horst Hottges   Luis Ubinas
Wolfgang Weber   Horacio Troche
Willi Schulz   Jorge Manicera
Karl-Heinz Schnellinger   Omar Caetano
Franz Beckenbauer   Pedro Rocha
Helmut Haller   Nestor Goncalvez
Uwe Seeler   Hector Salva
Siegfried Held   Julio Cortes
Lothar Emerich   Hector Silva
Wolfgang Overath   Domingo Perez

Referee: James Finney (England)
Linesmen: Hugh Philips (Scotland), Aly Kandil (UAR)
Attendance: 35,751 (£34,422)

Match 27, Goodison Park, Saturday 23 July

Portugal (2)5   North Korea (3)3
Eusebio 4 (2 pens)   Pak Seung Zin, Li Dong Woon
Augusto   Yang Sung Kook

PORTUGAL   NORTH KOREA

Jose Pereira   Li Chan Myung
Joao Morais   Lim Zoong Sun
Alexandre Baptista   Shin Yung Kyoo
Vicente Lucas   Ha Jung Won
Hilario Conceicao   Oh Yoon Kyung
Jaime Graca   Pak Seung Zin
Mario Coluna   Im Seung Hwi
Jose Augusto   Han Bong Zin
Eusebio Ferreira   Pak Doo Ik
Jose Torres   Li Dong Woon
Antonio Simoes   Yang Sung Kook

Referee: Menachem Ashkenasi (Israel)
Linesmen: Pierre Schwinte (France), Dr Karol Galba (Czechoslovakia)
Attendance: 51,780 (£48,749 5s 3d)

Match 28, Roker Park, Saturday 23 July

USSR (1)2   Hungary (0)1
Chislenko   Bene)
Porkujan

USSR

Lev Yashin
Vladimir Ponomarev
Albert Shesternev
Valeriy Voronin
Vasiliy Danilov
Iosif Sabo
Galimzjan Khusainov
Igor Chislenko
Anatoliy Banishevskiy
Eduard Malofeev
Valeriy Porkujan

HUNGARY

Jozsef Gelei
Beno Kaposzta
Gustav Szepesi-Szedunka
Kalman Meszoly
Sandor Matrai
Ferenc Sipos
Istvan Nagy
Ferenc Bene
Florian Albert
Janos Farkas
Gyula Rakosi

Referee: Juan Gardeazabal (Spain)
Linesmen: Joaquim Fernandes Campos (Portugal), Jose Maria Codesal (Uruguay)
Attendance: 26,844 (£23,364)

Semi-Finals

Match 29, Goodison Park, Monday 25 July

West Germany (1)2   USSR (0)1
(Haller, Beckenbauer)   (Porkujan)

WEST GERMANY

Hans Tilkowski
Friedel Lutz
Willi Schulz
Wolfgang Weber
Karl-Heinz Schnellinger
Franz Beckenbauer
Helmut Haller
Uwe Seeler
Siegfried Held
Wolfgang Overath
Lothar Emmerich

USSR

Lev Yashin
Vladimir Ponomarev
Albert Shesternev
Vasiliy Danilov
Valeriy Voronin
Iosif Sabo
Galimzjan Khusainov
Igor Chislenko
Anatoliy Banishevskiy
Eduard Malofeev
Valeriy Porkujan

Referee: Concetto Lo Bello (Italy)
Linesman: Juan Gardeazabal (Spain), Jose Maria Codesal (Uruguay)
Attendance: 43,921 (£47,051 9s 6d)

Match 30, Wembley Stadium, Tuesday 26 July

England (1)2   Portugal (0)1
Charlton, R. 2   Eusebio (pen.)

ENGLAND

Gordon Banks
George Cohen
John Charlton
Robert Moore
Ramon Wilson
Norbert Stiles
Robert Charlton
Alan Ball
Geoffrey Hurst

PORTUGAL

Jose Periera
Alberto Festa
Alexandre Baptista
Jose Carlos
Hilario Conceicao
Jaime Graca
Mario Coluna
Jose Augusto
Eusebio Ferreira

Roger Hunt
Martin Peters

Jose Torres
Antonio Simoes

Referee: Pierre Schwinte (France)
Linesmen: Konstantin Zecevic (Yugoslavia), Arturo Yamasaki (Peru)
Attendance: 94,493 (£133,933 11s 6d)

Third/Fourth Place Play-Off

Match 31, Wembley Stadium, Thursday 28 July

Portugal (1)2   USSR (1)1
Eusebio (pen.)   Malofeev)
Torres

PORTUGAL

USSR

Jose Pereira
Alberto Festa
Alexandre Baptista
Jose Carlos
Hilario Conceicao
Jaime Graca
Mario Coluna
Jose Augusto
Eusebio Ferreira
Jose Torres
Antonio Simoes

Lev Yashin
Vladimir Ponomarev
Murtaz Khurtsilava
Alexey Korneev
Vasiliy Danilov
Valeriy Voronin
Georgiy Sichinava
Slava Metreveli
Eduard Malofeev
Anatoliy Banishevskiy
Victor Serebrjannikov

Referee: Kenneth Dagnall (England)
Linesmen: Kevin Howley (England), Aly Kandil (UAR)
Attendance: 87,696 (£96,029 5s 0d)

The World Cup Final

Match 32, Wembley Stadium, Saturday 30 July

England (1)4   West Germany (1)2
Hurst 3, Peters   Haller, Weber

(After extra time – score after 90 minutes 2-2)

ENGLAND   WEST GERMANY

Gordon Banks   Hans Tilkowski
George Cohen   Horst Hottges
John Charlton   Willi Schulz
Robert Moore   Wolfgang Weber
Ramon Wilson   Karl-Heinz Schellinger
Norbert Stiles   Franz Beckenbauer
Robert Charlton   Helmut Haller
Alan Ball   Wolfgang Overath
Geoffrey Hurst   Siegfried Held
Roger Hunt   Uwe Seeler
Martin Peters   Lothar Emmerich

Referee: Gottfried Dienst (Switzerland)
Linesmen: Dr. Karol Galba (Czechoslovakia), Tofik Bakhramov (USSR)
Attendance: 96,924 (£204,805 – a world record for any football match)